LOSING FACE

LOSING FACE

A MEMOIR OF LOST IDENTITY AND SELF-DISCOVERY

KATHY TORPIE

HarperCollins*Publishers*

National Library of New Zealand Cataloguing-in-Publication Data

Torpie, Kathleen.
Losing face : a memoir of lost identity and self discovery / Kathleen
Torpie.
ISBN 1-86950-578-6
1. Disfigured persons—New Zealand—Biography. 2. Traffic accident
victims—New Zealand—Biography. I. Title.
362.197952092—dc 22

First published 2005
HarperCollins*Publishers* (New Zealand) Limited
P.O. Box 1, Auckland

The opinions expressed in this book are those of the author or of
other persons and are not those of the publisher: the publisher has
no reasonable cause to believe that the opinions set out in the book
are not the genuine opinions of the author or of those other persons.

The author and publisher thank copyright holders for granting
permission to reproduce copyright material.
Close to the Bone: Life Threatening Illness and the Search for Meaning,
Dr Jean Bolen, Scribner, 1996
A Leg to Stand On, Dr Oliver Sacks, Picador/Pan Books, 1986

ISBN 1 86950 578 6

Cover design by Darren Holt, Harper Collins Design Studio
Cover image by Getty Images
Internal text design and typesetting by Springfield West
Printed by Griffin Press, Australia, on 79gsm Bulky Paperback

Dedication

To my friends and family who supported me beyond my wildest dreams. Without you I would not have survived emotionally.

To all of the medical and health professionals whose combined skills saved my life, my limbs, my face and my ability to function. Without you I would not have survived physically nor been able, finally, to feel at home in my body again.

And to my 'Guardian Angel', the spirit that never left my side even as I raged and fell into despair. Without you I would never have found my way back to my self.

One does not become enlightened by imagining figures of light, but by making the darkness conscious.

— Carl Jung

If you bring forth what is within you, what you bring forth will save you. If you do not bring forth what is within you, what you do not bring forth will destroy you.

— Jesus

Contents

Introduction

We know that we are spiritual beings on a human path rather than human beings who may be on a spiritual path.

— Dr Jean Shindoa Bolen, *Close To The Bone*

Everyone shares a fear of 'losing face', of losing all that defines us as unique individuals in the world and of losing the status that comes with that image. In 1994, as the result of a head-on collision with a drunk driver, I literally lost my face and all that had previously defined who I was. Though my body survived, I felt as though I had died. Thus began the long journey of recovering myself — the 'me' behind the face, the body, the personality and achievements.

There are many well-known myths and religious parables that portray that part of the human journey where one must descend into the darkness, the abyss or the underworld before transformation is possible. This descent usually involves the stripping away of all that previously protected us from the dark, the unacceptable, and that which we fear most. Coming face to face with our naked vulnerability, we are humbled and given an opportunity for growth on a level that is not otherwise possible. We lose our innocence and will never again be the same. Yet when we dare — or are forced by circumstances — to face the darkness, allowing our illusions to be stripped away, new understandings become available that can change our relationship with ourselves, with others and with life itself.

In the story that is the foundation of Christianity, Jesus was literally stripped naked and defiled before he was hung on a cross, buried in a cave, and was later resurrected and ascended to heaven. Buddha descended into the moral excesses that he had previously condemned before he re-emerged enlightened and no longer in fear of those temptations. The Hindu goddess Kali, the goddess of death and rebirth, is worshipped by millions who recognise that destruction is essential to the process of creation and that both are cause for celebration. In Greek mythology, the maiden Persephony was abducted by Hades, lord of the underworld, as she gathered flowers in a field. Thereafter each year she was released from the underworld for that period of time we call spring. Hers is a reminder of the continuing cyclical nature of descent and renewal.

My favourite such story is the ancient Sumerian myth of Inanna's descent into the underworld. It is a story depicting the need to allow the death of who we are — or believe ourselves to be — in order to free who we can become.

Before the ego can be safely relinquished it must be made fully aware of all that it keeps hidden in the shadows of the unconscious. The process is long and arduous. It demands that sufficient time be given both to the shedding of the old and to the integration of the new.

Inanna was a Sumerian goddess and queen of heaven and earth. When she discovers that her sister goddess, Ereshkigal, queen of the underworld, is suffering, Inanna decides to visit her. But descending into the underworld is neither easy nor straightforward. In order to enter the underworld domain of Ereshkigal, Inanna must pass through seven gates. At each gate she must relinquish some symbol of her power and prestige until, at last, she enters the underworld naked.

Symbolising the outer persona that we present to the world, Inanna is stripped of all of her illusions until she stands naked before Ereshkigal, the hidden and disowned part of herself condemned to the shadowy underworld. When Inanna finally passes naked and humbled into the underworld home of her sister, Ereshkigal strikes her dead and hangs her body on a hook, where it begins to decompose into a slab of green meat. Only then, having died as who she was and knowing the darkness and suffering of Ereshkigal as her own, is Inanna able to resurface from the dark underworld transformed.

I found the myth of Inanna an affirmation of my own process. For years after the accident, I remained stuck in the loss of my identity, waiting for a new me to be born. The journey wasn't over when I was stripped naked of all I previously held myself to be. Being 'hung up on the hook' was, for me, the inactive and powerless and humbling time of waiting. Not for rescue or release. By then I knew that wasn't possible. I was waiting for the new me to take shape, for re-formation, integration, and surfacing. Before that was possible, I had to go into the depths of my being, to recognise and own all that lay behind the image I had previously worn and held to be true.

Like a person trapped in an eddy, trying to escape, only to be drawn back in time and again, I realised that the only way out was to go down. Finding my way back into the current of life meant surrendering myself to the dark waters beneath the surface, where I encountered both my humanity and my sanctity before resurfacing with greater compassion for myself and for the human condition. It wasn't wisdom on my part that showed me the way. It was the pure exhaustion of fighting so long and so hard to emerge victorious (and back in 'control') that finally led me to surrender to the darkness.

You don't literally need to lose your physical face to be confronted with the crisis of having to redefine your place in the world. It is an experience shared by those made redundant in their work, by new parents or full-time mothers whose children have left home, by the newly divorced, by menopausal women, and by a vast number of adolescents making the transition from childhood to adulthood. Every transition that forces us to make essential changes in the way that we live our lives is an opportunity to rediscover who we really are behind the faces that we so convincingly wear.

The individual details of our stories may vary. But the archetypal descent and return is a journey we are all given many opportunities to embark on in our lives.

1

Vulnerable? Who, me?

I'm still trying to find my way from my past to my future, but feel more willing to let the universe show me the way. This is new and I'm awkward at it. The instinct to control dies hard.

I had never truly known that I was vulnerable. With the exception perhaps of a broken heart or pain inflicted by an unkind word, I had somehow managed to retain well into my forties the arrogant belief that I was invincible, that I could do or be whatever I wished so long as I wanted it badly enough. In some naive way, I believed that I was in control and that if life didn't go as I wanted, it was only because I had miscalculated in some way. In one breathless instant as I saw the headlights of a drunk driver suddenly appear at high speed from around the corner, in my lane, I understood how very wrong I was.

I didn't let go of control easily. In that stunned moment, as the headlights closed in on me, I refused to accept the inevitable. Instead, I somehow managed to assess my options, looking for a way out. How quickly it all happened. At first, denial. ('No! This can't be!') I was on a narrow unlit country road with headlights hurtling towards me in my lane. The car behind me had been tailgating for some time. A quick look told me he was still there. I couldn't hit the brakes! I bargained. I begged. ('Please! God!') There was no shoulder to pull off the road or even out of the way. I knew instantly that if I swerved into the other lane and he corrected at the last moment, I could kill us all. Finally, came acceptance. There was nothing I could do! It was the longest moment of my life and yet not long enough to take another breath before the life I had known for forty-seven years came to an abrupt halt.

It ended in blinding white light that oddly enough I remember as beautiful. This wasn't a vision of God or heaven. It was the headlights of an old English-made car with a heavy chassis and a very drunk driver descending upon me. I will never know the details of what happened in that instant. I can only guess from the photos of the cars and my injuries that the impact propelled me forward, crushing my legs as the seat tore loose, catapulting me, strapped shoulder and waist, into the steering wheel. My head smashed against the cross bar of the steering wheel, bending it and shattering every bone of my face between my lower jaw and forehead. As my car spun from the impact, the car behind me smashed into my driver's door and I was left sandwiched in twisted metal up to my shoulders in the dark and terrible stillness that followed.

It took half an hour for a rescue team to arrive and an hour to cut me out of the car. All of this time I was conscious and fighting for the control I had relied on all of my life. Gratefully, I don't remember pain. Only a terror beyond anything I can even attempt to describe. I was helpless. Trapped, broken and alone, waiting for help to arrive. Part of me panicking. Silently begging, praying, for this not to be so. Another part soothing, comforting, reassuring 'It will be OK.' Reminding me to not struggle. To focus on breathing. To wait for help. I knew somehow that I would live. But that I couldn't do it alone. It was that total loss of control, of complete helplessness, that was most frightening. Yet, as I waited for help to arrive, I discovered that in some strange way I wasn't alone, that something was there with me, something that was unbroken, that took care of me and got me through the initial crisis.

Weeks later, the head of the rescue team visited me in the hospital and told me how strong and brave he thought I'd been. But it wasn't 'me'. I was terrified — as much by my total helplessness as by the extent of my injuries that I couldn't yet begin to fathom. Perhaps it was a self-nurturing part of my own psyche — my 'inner parent' — that calmed and reassured me, that took control on my behalf. Perhaps it was my 'guardian angel'. Or even God. Whatever it was had probably always been there with me. I'd just been too busy running my own life to have ever noticed.

Had anyone attempted to describe me prior to the accident the words 'independent' and 'adventurous' would likely have been included in their description. I spent my early twenties ski-bumming in Vermont, where snow storms were a cause for celebration and sub-zero temperatures only meant that the lift lines were shorter. It mattered not one bit that I left a well-paid teaching job in a prestigious suburb of Boston for a waitressing job in a ski resort. What mattered was that I could ski every day. By the second year, I had my own shop on the mountain where I made and sold silver jewellery to tourists. And when in the third year ski conditions were bad, I decided to close my shop, head to Florida and learn to sail instead. I hitchhiked as a cook and apprentice sailor on yachts through the Caribbean and the Panama Canal and across the Pacific Ocean. I spent weeks in the Galapagos Islands on an 82-foot yacht where I swam with seals, visited a beach deserted but for flocks of pink flamingos, and hiked on the empty moonscape of volcanic islands where giant iguanas roamed. By the time I arrived in New Zealand I could both sail and do basic navigation. I had intended to continue around the world, but New Zealand stole my heart. It was 1974 and I was twenty-seven years old.

I toured New Zealand from top to bottom before finding a job. Thereafter my adventures were limited to my generous New Zealand holidays and weekends — hiking, camping, kayaking, sailing. I met my fortieth birthday defiantly by learning to skydive. When the moment came to jump, I didn't quite have the courage to throw myself at the ground 3000 feet below with arms and legs outstretched, as I had been instructed. I just let go and the weight of the pack carrying my chute flipped me over backwards. To my horror, the chute opened, but the lines were twisted, making it impossible to direct my landing.

I remember the instructor's voice in my earphones telling me what I had to do to untangle the lines. 'I can't!' I shouted to the rapidly decreasing space that lay between me and the earth. 'I'm not strong enough!' Then a voice in my head (perhaps the same one that calmed me in the car seven years later) took control on my behalf. 'You have to.' I threw my weight with all the force I could gather in the opposite direction to the twisted lines, managing to untangle the lines and land safely. Then, to everyone's surprise, I insisted on going right back up to do it again. I wanted to get it right and not be left with lingering fear. This time, against all my instincts I threw my arms open wide as I leapt toward the earth. It was a glorious experience!

Somehow, in all of the risky things I've done in my life I have managed to stay just a few steps ahead of having to confront my vulnerability or my limits. Looking back, I think that the fierceness of my independence was really no more than a hiding place for my fear of dependence. But I didn't know that at the time. So, when I found myself trapped and helpless in the wreckage of my car I knew no other response than to act strong and to fight for my life.

And fight I did! I'm told by the fireman who cut me out of the car that, although my jaw had been snapped off by the impact, I managed to assist him with my rescue by indicating what effect his manoeuvres were having on me. In critical care fear took over. Emergency staff cut open my belly to check for internal bleeding. I didn't understand why they cut my already torn and broken body and, even in my critical condition, I was unwilling to give up control. I was scared! And when I'm scared I fight. Though they were working to save my life, the impersonal, clinical takeover of emergency procedures only served to intensify my fear. I hadn't been able to protect myself from the accident and now my guard was up against any possible further danger. In that state I was incapable of relinquishing without question what little control I might have had left. And I was equally incapable of exercising any kind of control at all. We were each battling to save my life — they to keep my body alive and me to keep some sense of my *self* alive. They succeeded. I did not. That was to come later. Much later.

Many people have since told me how lucky I was not to have died in the accident. Yet, in many ways, I *had* died in that accident. Everything I had based my sense of 'self' on was gone. My body, my face, my spirit, my sense of safety in the world and confidence in myself would never again be the same. The life that was saved by the hard work of so many medical professionals that night and in the following weeks of intensive care was not the life I had known until then. That life was over. What the critical and intensive care staff did for me — all they possibly could do for me — was to give me the opportunity to create a new life and eventually a new sense of my self.

2

Becoming a patient

Choices have come to feel more ominous with the growing fear that I might waste what no longer feels boundless. This life is finite. It is no longer simply a choice of what I will do first. Now it's either/or.

Ironically, the accident happened during one of those particularly good times in my life. My early forties had been an unsettling period of transition, of 'mid-life crisis', in which I sought new direction in my life. At forty-two I took a year off work, bought an around-the-world ticket and a new backpack. Storing all of my belongings and renting out my house, I went in search of the freedom and adventure I had once known. What I found instead was a lot of very young backpackers smoking dope and sunbathing naked on beaches close to Buddhist and Hindu villages. The indigenous people seemed so overwhelmed by tourism that it was difficult to be accepted by them as anything other than a potential customer. I returned, disillusioned, to my full-time job and responsibilities as a home-owner.

Then I discovered what was called 'New Paradigm Thinking'. From physics to economics, the connection was being made that all things are interdependent and interrelated. Reading Fritjof Capra's *The Tao of Physics*, I discovered that others far more knowledgeable than I were thinking along the same lines that I had been struggling to clarify. I quit my job and set off to the famous Esalen Institute in California and other New Age centres throughout the USA to live and work in exchange for my room, board and tuition. I anticipated chopping vegetables in the kitchen of Esalen with the mindfulness of a Zen monk while discussing the implications of this exciting new thinking with fellow volunteers. Instead, conversation focused on who was sleeping with whom and who was at fault in the local politics of the institute.

Discovering that I could neither reclaim my past not surge headlong into some idealised future was oddly liberating. I returned to New Zealand, by now my home for twenty years, knowing that all I had was the present and believing that I could make of it whatever I chose. I returned, not to my cosy little Victorian cottage in the city, but to wild, windy Muriwai Beach on New Zealand's rugged west coast, where I made the commitment to myself to write daily. I spent my days writing and soaking up the expansive sea view, then taking long, delicious walks on the beach. I did t'ai chi and yoga and planned kayaking trips with friends. I was feeling happy with life again and confident that my future would unfold as it should in its own time. At forty-seven my body still moved with the power and ease of a well-tuned car and I considered the lines around my eyes a reminder of the laughter and sunshine in my life.

I completed my first feature article in my new role as a full-time freelance journalist and dropped it in the mailbox, full of hope. I was on my way to a dinner reunion with other aspiring writers that I'd met that summer at a journalism class, and Paul, our tutor. We were to meet in Mission Bay, a wealthy suburb on Auckland's Pacific harbour forty-five minutes from the pounding surf and black sands of my new home on the Tasman coast. It seemed an entire world away and I was torn about whether or not to go. But it was well worth it. At dinner several of us decided to form a writers' support group. Paul praised my writing and encouraged me to continue, offering me a good deal on a second-hand computer to mark my decision to write full time. When, at last, the evening drew to a close, a few of us lingered in the parking lot, not wanting the evening to end. I was offered a bed in Auckland to save me the long drive back. It was tempting, but I declined. I was excited that my decision to write full time was so well supported and wanted to get to work first thing in the morning. It was on the way home that night — only minutes from my door — that all my plans came to an abrupt halt.

In that instant, every bone of my facial skeleton was shattered. The radiography report on my facial fractures describes the horror in clinical terms: 'The markedly comminuted [fragmented] nature of this fracture is best demonstrated by visualisation of the film as the report cannot clearly cover every bony fragment of this grossly comminuted facial injury.' As my face struck the steering wheel, my upper jaw snapped off so that it hung 'like an unattached dental plate', according to one surgeon. My ribs were broken and both lungs punctured. The bones of my left forearm and wrist broke and my legs were so severely fractured that broken bones tore through the skin. One section of my lower leg was reduced to splinters. The knee cap was shattered beyond repair and a huge chunk of flesh torn from my leg below the knee, leaving a hole that could be covered only by removing part of my calf muscle and placing it over the hole. I didn't know these details at the time. I knew only that I was broken and that I was alone.

Probably every person living alone has entertained at some time or other the nightmare of being critically injured or killed and no one close knowing. It is an aloneness not easy to imagine and harder to experience. Because I had just moved to the beach and because I was single and living on the other side of the world from my family in the United States, the address on my driver's licence was of no use to notify my next of kin. It was only by pure luck that a policeman recognised the street name on my licence as the same street that a woman he knew from Victim Support lived on. She was my neighbour and, by chance, I had just given her my new phone number and address at the beach. It was she who called my mother and notified my friends.

Alone in her apartment half a world away, my eighty-year-old mother received the phone call that every parent dreads. She was told that the damage was serious and that it was unknown if my leg could be saved or even if I would survive such extensive surgery in my condition. As surgeons struggled for twelve hours to piece my limbs back together with metal rods and plates and friends stood vigil at the hospital, my mother and two of my sisters struggled to update passports and caught the first available flight to New Zealand, not knowing what they would encounter when they landed.

When they arrived two days later, exhausted and distraught, they were confronted with the horror of seeing me in critical care. What had been my face was a massive swelling without form. My eyes were swollen shut and my jaw wired closed. Tubes and machines performed all of my major functions. I couldn't move, couldn't speak, couldn't see, couldn't eat or drink or control elimination. I couldn't even breathe for myself. A tube had been placed through a hole cut in my throat to fill my lungs with air. Another placed in my urethra to drain urine. IV lines in my arms and chest supplied fluids, nutrition and medication. Beeping monitors were attached to measure my pulse and the air in my blood while faceless strangers took readings, changed tubes, gave injections and wrote notes in my chart. Trapped in this horror, my hearing seemed supersonic, searching through all the noises of a busy critical care unit for any information about what was happening to me! I desperately wanted to be included in whatever that was. I wanted someone who loved me to be there, to be my advocate and protector in this alien and frightening environment.

When my family arrived I immediately felt relieved, glad to hand the control of my care over to them. I was exhausted by self-imposed hyper-vigilance against any further danger, by trying, as I have always done, to be stronger than I really was. Even though my friends had loved and supported me beyond my wildest dreams as they waited for my family's arrival (one even sitting by my bedside all night so that I would not wake from surgery alone), it was family that I needed at that moment and that I clung to for support. They could protect me and see that I got the best care.

Soon after they arrived, I was horrified to learn that I was being transferred from one of the best hospitals in New Zealand, one close to my home and friends, to another hospital that was run down and in a poor area on the outskirts of the city. I felt horribly abandoned by the very people who had saved my life. I had made it safely to the hospital and had survived twelve hours of surgery. My family and close friends were nearby and now I wanted only to rest and recover. I felt certain that I was too sick to be transferred. Even though I was heavily drugged, the idea of change, now, after all I had been through, was too much.

But move me they did. It didn't matter that I held private health insurance. All accidents in New Zealand are covered by government accident insurance and are automatically sent to public, teaching hospitals to be treated by whoever is on call in any particular specialty. I was still in need of extensive plastic surgery and since that department was at the other hospital, I was moved — tubes, machines, and all — from Auckland Hospital's critical care unit to intensive care at Middlemore Hospital forty minutes south of Auckland. My family was helpless to do anything but beg me to calm down and cooperate. It was the first of many times that I felt overwhelmed by the burden of being asked to protect my caregivers from experiencing my distress. To put on a brave face, a compliant face, though I felt neither brave nor compliant. I wanted to howl in terror and rage at being moved for the convenience of the system. I wanted someone who knew and loved me to defend and protect me in this impersonal environment. But this only added to their own feelings of helplessness and distress.

Each day every one of us puts on a 'face' for the world, hiding the unacceptable from view. It's often so habitual that it's unconscious. I was about to learn just how much energy it actually takes to maintain an acceptable image for the comfort of others at the price of one's authenticity. It was energy diverted from my healing.

3

A new face and invisibility

The difference between compassion and pity is that compassion is based on connection and pity on separateness. I imagine both the compassionate and the pitying think, 'Thank God that's not me.' The difference is that the compassionate person remembers that it just as easily could have been.

A young plastic surgeon with gentle eyes came to examine me shortly after I was transferred from Auckland hospital. I could see only through the slits of swollen eye sockets, but I recall feeling for the first time since the accident that here was a doctor actually looking at me! It was the first time in this nightmare of medical interventions that I felt myself visible as a person. As his eyes searched my face measuring and assessing, I watched. Taking my chin between his thumb and forefinger, his focus widened. He seemed to take in all of me. To see the person lying there. He said something to me then. I can't remember what. A gentle reassurance perhaps. What I remember is the simple but profound feeling of being personally acknowledged. I had no face. I knew that. Enough people had spoken of it around me. Presumably they assumed that because I couldn't open my eyes, I couldn't hear either. But this man seemed to see beyond that, to see me. And I felt sure that in his face I saw not pity, but compassion. I felt so grateful that I wanted to cry.

A few days later this same man cut me from ear to ear across the top of my head and literally peeled off my face. Then he painstakingly pieced the bones of my face back together like a jigsaw puzzle and held them in place with metal plates and screws without leaving any visible scars. I'd come in without anything left of my facial skeleton above the jaw. No nose. Nothing but fragments. Twelve hours later I re-emerged with the framework of my new face in place.

My sister could resist no longer. 'Aren't you even curious about how you look?' I wasn't. Some say that you are never given more than you can cope with at any moment. I believe that's true. I could somehow cope with the idea of being without a face. In the weeks of silence, unable to speak, I had journeyed to a place far from the superficial world of personal image. It was an interior world that required no face. When I could open my eyes enough to see the faces of friends and family who came to visit, I saw them looking at *me*, not at the horror of my appearance. I saw only their love.

So, when my sister placed a large mirror in front of me, I wasn't prepared. The face I saw was wide and flat with just the tip of a shortened nose. It was horribly swollen and the left eye sat low and at an angle on my cheek. It was a miracle of modern medicine that the surgeon was able to recreate a face where, in the damaged region, there had been no bony pieces larger than two centimetres. But it wasn't attractive. And it wasn't me. The last time I had looked in a mirror, only a few weeks before, was on my way out the door on the night of the accident. I was dressed up and looking good. Now, lying in a hospital bed, I closed my eyes then slowly opened them and looked again, half expecting to see someone more familiar reflected back at me. But it was the same swollen, bewildered-looking face whose blank eyes returned my stare. I felt no horror, only a detached curiosity and perhaps some compassion for the stranger in the mirror. It wasn't me. I was trapped on the inside, silent and unseen. In the following months I returned to the mirror hundreds of times looking for the face that I had always found there, unwilling to believe that it was truly lost.

This sense of invisibility remained with me for much of my early days in hospital. Staff and family alike talked about me as though I wasn't present or couldn't hear, simply because I couldn't speak and my eyes were swollen shut. Nurses often held personal conversations in my presence as they watched over me. I was heavily drugged and slipped in and out of consciousness frequently, so that I was confused and disoriented when I woke to the sound of nurses discussing their personal relationships as if I wasn't there. I often imagined myself a captive of some sort and these my captors. I knew that the drugs were having this effect on me, yet I couldn't shake the fear that came from the combination of my own inability to see and the sense I had of being unseen and unacknowledged.

I was desperate for soothing physical contact. Most contact by medical staff was purely functional and often painful — injections, drip lines, blood pressure, pulse, temperature, oxygen level, bathing, and, of course, cleaning and changing me when the bowels I couldn't control were released. I was experiencing all of this with the mind of a proud and previously independent adult.

I sensed from their touch which caregivers were offended or irritated when I soiled myself, which were self-conscious about washing me, and which were reluctant even to experience the painful connection of our common humanity, to know that this could just as easily have happened to them or to someone they love. I struggled to work out whose hands were washing me or changing dressings and drips or monitoring vital signs. The touch I received was often intimate or invasive by its very nature, yet always impersonal, professional and efficient. I yearned for gentle touch and sensed that it too was essential to my survival. Occasionally the touch I received was so full of gentle compassion that I leaned into it, hungry for more. At other times, particularly for invasive procedures like inserting drips or administering shots, I allowed a numb, dissociative passivity to take over.

I had no control of my bowels and, even in a critical condition, felt humiliated each time liquid stools escaped with a squelching sound from my body. I will never forget soiling the bed right after a male nurse had finished changing my sheets. I cringed in shame and was met with a gentle voice reassuring me that it was not my fault, as he patiently proceeded to wash and change me all over again. Did he know how much this simple kindness meant to me, still means to me? Each time he was assigned to my case he would begin by touching my shoulder and greeting me by name, leaning close to my face so that I could see him through the slits of my eyes. And, always when his shift was over, he would gently say goodbye. The single occasion when I heard an audible sigh coming from an attending nurse who was obviously annoyed when my bowels released involuntarily is just as memorable. The shame I felt was excruciating. Every small kindness and every small slight from my caregivers seemed magnified by the enormity of the vulnerability I felt. Even now memories of 'insignificant' events can rekindle deep gratitude or anger.

Having my hair washed in bed was one of those events. After what probably amounted to a week in intensive care lying half-propped up in my bed like an infant in a stroller — my head lolling to one side and my bandage drooping over my eyes, unable to shift position for myself — an angel in a nurse's uniform washed my hair. I still can't figure out how she managed it as I lay in bed. She was gentle, I remember. And she talked to me as she worked. This was the nurturing touch I craved. The transformation in my sense of dignity was equalled only by the transformation of my spirits. I remember how important the rituals of personal hygiene were to my sense of wellbeing every day after that until I left the hospital more than three months later.

Similarly, one seemingly harmless bit of black humour became something of a crisis. I was heavily drugged, enough so that I felt no pain. But I did have sensation. My genital area felt puffed and swollen. With all of the antibiotics I was receiving, I knew I probably had a vaginal yeast infection, but I didn't know how to communicate that. So when a nurse was washing me and superficially passed over my genital area, I tried to point to that area. Sure enough I had a flaming infection! The curtain around my bed was closed, but I felt horribly exposed and vulnerable. People walked in and out all the time and didn't always close the curtain completely. I attempted to communicate that I felt exposed and vulnerable. But when I was given a pad and pen to try to communicate, my letters came out backwards, I forgot words and I couldn't spell. What got communicated was that I was terribly anxious and seemed to others to be afraid of some kind of sexual interference!

Someone made a snide remark within my hearing about my genitals. I knew it was only a joke and not intended for my ears. But the idea that my life was in the hands of anyone who could joke so disrespectfully about me in my helpless condition made me panic. I didn't want family to leave my side. I tried to ask for a patient advocate but couldn't for the life of me remember the word 'advocate'. Staff insisted that I was having 'paranoid delusions' from the drugs. A psychiatrist was called in to assess me. Amazingly, she asked the questions I had learned so many years ago as a novice counsellor when assessing patients for severe mental illness. Did I know who I was, where I was, and the day of the week? There isn't even a difference between day and night in intensive care, let alone anything to indicate what day of the week it is! Luckily it was Mother's Day and I told her so. She laughed and confirmed in my clinical notes that I was not suffering from drug-induced delusions. I was sane and that was the end of it. Nothing was ever said again about the real reason behind my 'paranoia'.

4

Getting worse and deciding to live

Dying is nothing to fear. It can be the most wonderful experience of your life.
— Elisabeth Kübler-Ross

Defeat the fear of death and welcome the death of fear.
— G. Gordon Liddy

I spent a total of three weeks in intensive care where my condition worsened before it slowly began to improve. Because my lungs had been punctured by broken ribs, holes had been cut in my upper chest walls to release air trapped in the chest cavity, air that otherwise may have compressed or collapsed my lungs. The openings in my chest wall and the hole in my throat for the respirator made me particularly susceptible to lung infection. My lungs eventually became so severely infected that, unable to sit up or call out for help, I found myself lying in silent horror several times as my lungs filled with fluid. It felt like I was drowning.

Whenever this happened, the ventilator would disconnect from the hole in my throat, blowing oxygen uselessly across my neck. The terror of these moments was matched only by the helpless rage of not knowing if anyone was witness to my silent desperation, could see that I was suffocating! How could they allow this to happen? Didn't they care? I had no way of calling for help. I could do nothing but hope that someone was there, that someone would notice and would rescue me. A nurse was always close at hand, of course. But because I couldn't see — and because no one had thought to tell me — I didn't know that I was never alone. I never knew if anyone was aware or would respond in time. All of my worst fears about being dependent and helpless seemed to be proving true. Each time my breathing tube dislodged from my throat, another tube had to be forced down my throat to suction my lungs before the ventilator could be replaced to supply my next breath. Each time it took more effort to recover. I knew that I was getting weaker. Dependent on machines to keep me alive and breathe for me, I felt my own capacity and will to live diminishing.

It was during one of these episodes when the tube disconnected that I believe I suffered cardiac failure. Struggling for air and panicked when I could get none, hands held me still as a tube was forced through the hole in my throat to suction my lungs. But my last breath of air was long ago. Too long, it seemed, to wait while they suctioned me. There was no more air! Eventually, too exhausted to struggle any longer, I let go . . . and experienced a sense of relief beyond any attempts I might make to describe it. I felt an enormous release and with it, a sudden expansion so extraordinary that it seemed as though the infinite had opened up before me. All that I had ever known was no more than a tiny, insignificant dot in the spaciousness that I found myself a part of. Yet everything was somehow familiar, remembered. It was like waking abruptly from a turbulent dream to the sweet knowledge that it was only a dream, that I was back in the real world of all that is familiar. From this perspective I experienced an overwhelmingly tender compassion, unlike anything I'd ever known before (or since), towards the sweet innocence of the human condition with all of its petty concerns. How like small children we all were!

Though I felt no physical pain, I was acutely aware of the pain and distress that my death would cause family and close friends, whose perspective was now so different from my own. I 'knew' without thought, that I was not this body and that its demise was no more tragic than being roused abruptly from an unfinished dream. Yet those who loved me didn't know — couldn't know — this simple truth. I felt something like a mother's compassion when witnessing her small child's bewilderment and grief at the first loss of a friend or the death of a pet — remembering the acute pain of her own first experience of loss yet knowing too how insignificant it truly was in the scheme of an entire lifetime. The distress of those who would grieve my loss elicited such love and compassion in me that it became more relevant that I survive. So that's what I did. Almost before I could fully register the sweet relief of abruptly 'waking up' to all that was real and familiar, I dropped back into my nightmare. Suddenly everything abruptly contracted. Where there had been compassion and acceptance, there was only fear, pain, and a determined struggle to survive. Ever since that moment I have yearned to re-experience that blissful, all-consuming compassion and utter lack of fear. But the tiny dot of my life with its own petty concerns continues to obscure everything else, even the infinite. At times I have grieved that loss more deeply than any other.

Soon after that incident, I indicated that I wanted to get off the ventilator. I wanted to try to breathe for myself. I mimed with my one good arm that I wanted to write a message. A pad of paper was laid on my stomach and a pen placed in my hand. With all my concentration I wrote 'PLEASE'. There was much consulting among medical staff. I had not breathed unassisted for three weeks. I had undergone two twelve-hour operations and suffered a serious lung infection. Yet I somehow knew that the longer I depended on a machine to breathe for me, the less capable I was of having the strength to breathe for myself. 'PLEASE!' To my mind, I was begging for my life.

I've always been a fiercely independent person, an independence born of a deep-rooted fear of helplessness. The accident had thrown me back into the total dependence of a newborn infant. As I took my first slow breath that day, consciously drawing air into my lungs and releasing it, unsure of the next breath, I felt a sense of wonder and of pride. I had to make an effort to fill my lungs and was rewarded with a sense of expansiveness. As my upper chest filled with air, I was aware of my shoulder blades gently rolling back, almost like the wings of a bird. As I exhaled, and my lungs contracted, the wings were drawn back in. I 'flew' like that for what seemed like hours while nurses and machines monitored my progress. Then I tired and the respirator was turned back on.

Whether or not my lungs would have become infected had I not been placed, with wounds that opened directly to my lungs, in a bed next to an elderly woman in critical condition from a lung infection, I will never know. It's one of those ironies of life that the daughter of that elderly woman, who was about my age, befriended my own elderly mother as the two of them sat side by side at our beds watching over us — mother and daughter, waiting and hoping, as we drifted in and out of consciousness. When my sisters had to return to the States two weeks later, leaving my mother alone in a strange country in the worst of circumstances, my fellow patient's kind daughter invited my mother to stay with their family. 'We've got a mother's bedroom at our house that isn't occupied at the moment,' she offered. My mother lived with this generous Maori family in South Auckland for six weeks, probably learning more about Maoritanga (the Maori way) than most foreign visitors to New Zealand ever get to experience. Months later, long after my mother had returned to the States, I was visited in my hospital ward by the woman whose room my mother had occupied and her daughter. Her daughter and my mother, strangers of a different race, different nationality, and different economic means, had filled in for critically ill family members who until that moment had never met.

5

Early milestones

*It was as though a new me was conceived in an act
of unspeakable violence. A 'me' forced to begin at
the very beginning . . . with the first breath.*

Once off the respirator, breathing quickly became second
nature and I soon lost touch with the gentle sensation
of the rising and falling of my breath. My eyes had opened
enough that I could finally see the environment that had
until now been limited to sounds and physical sensations,
although I suffered from a kind of rotating double vision
that turned my visual world into a kaleidoscope of moving
images for many weeks to come. I couldn't watch television
or read, but I did occasionally get a secret laugh at the comic
distortions of people's faces that my double vision created
and that only I could see.

Shortly before I left intensive care, a doctor came in

to remove the respirator permanently and to close off the hole in my throat. As he prepared to do this, he told me to press against the wound in my throat and try to talk. I didn't understand. Talk? I had assumed that my vocal cords were cut when the hole was made in my throat and that I would never talk again. I had lived in a world of mute silence for three weeks and had reluctantly come to accept this as my future. The doctor took my hand and pressed my fingers against my throat.

'Go ahead, just talk,' he said.

But I was too shocked. I had lost my voice and now I couldn't find it. 'I'm scared! I'm scared!' A high-pitched nasal voice burst forth. 'I want my Mommie! Where's my Mommie?' Was that me? Mommie? I hadn't called her Mommie since I was a small child. But, in that moment, I was a small child. And 'Mommie' was exactly who I needed.

The whole world changed, it seemed, once I could talk again. For the first time those caregivers who had looked after a silent broken body were confronted with a human being who could now assert her personality. I could ask for what I needed and ask all the questions that had filled my silent mind for those three weeks. I voiced my thanks to those nurses who had cared for me with tenderness and respect, so grateful finally to be able to introduce myself. And, not unlike a child, I found myself saying things to win favour with those nurses who seemed cold or impersonal but upon whom I still depended.

Mom was away having a coffee when I got my voice back. But when she returned to be told that I was now talking, she responded with the same proud delight of any parent whose toddler has just spoken her first word. We cried together and I finally got to tell her what it meant to me that she had come so far at her age to be with me. Her love for me was so tangible that the little girl that had been reawakened in me was awed to feel so loved. And the woman in me was able, at last, to return that love in full. In the years since the accident, that love has continued to grow and to heal a spirit wounded long before the accident.

I probably feared my mother as much as I needed her when I was little. I think I feared her because I needed her. Mom was struggling just to cope with the demands of providing a rapidly growing brood with the mothering that she experienced so little of in her own childhood. Her father had abandoned her young mother after World War I, leaving my grandmother to raise (and support) four young girls alone. Mom and her sisters were shuffled here and there as her mother tried to cope. By the time she was fourteen years old, my mother left home to share an apartment with her married sister and went to work to support herself.

It was right after World War II that I was born. My mother had two young toddlers at the time and was pregnant again before I was nine months old. I'm told that I was brought home from the hospital to a draughty beach cottage that my parents rented in the bitter New York winter. Eventually we moved into our own house. Like most other families in the western world we children were demanding of attention. More demanding — at least in my case — than my mother could easily tolerate. She was often irritable and, I suspect, overwhelmed by the constant demands placed on her. Like most kids, I took it personally, sure that she didn't really love me. So I pretended — all my life — that I didn't really need her. Apparently I never fooled anyone but myself. All these years later I was again as dependent and vulnerable as I had been as an infant. Only this time I could see my mother's love for me clearly and could embrace it with all my heart. It was a milestone as worthy of celebration as any other.

Now that I was off the respirator, I quickly graduated from intensive care to a private room in the plastic surgery ward where the surgeon would oversee my care. My mother bought me two elegant nightgowns to mark the occasion. No more open-backed, white or blue hospital-issued gowns for me. From now on I had a choice between a satin nightshirt and a delicate Victorian-style nightgown. I had survived, and now all that was left was for me to begin physiotherapy and give my bones time to heal. I was eager to begin my rehabilitation and to begin to take charge of my life again.

For every loss I experienced, there were milestones in my recovery that transformed the mundane into the miraculous. In the three weeks since being plunged by fate from an independent lifestyle into the abyss of complete helplessness, I had journeyed from death to birth with my first unassisted breath. I was now working my way through infancy. Finally able to sit up by myself and take liquids by mouth, I had control of both my bladder and my bowels! These apparently tiny achievements were a source of great pride for me. They were markers of my journey, however slow, back to independence. In another two weeks the wiring of my jaw would be removed and I would at long last be able to eat solid food, though at first only purées and foods that I could 'chew' with my tongue against my palate. It would be even longer before I could manage the real thing. But the crisis was over and all would be well from now on. Or so I thought. Little did I realise all that still lay ahead of me! As I said my goodbyes to the charge nurse of the intensive care unit, I offered to visit every now and then to volunteer my services as a counsellor to grieving families while I underwent my physical rehabilitation. She looked at me strangely, almost tenderly, and replied, 'You just take care of yourself, Kathy.'

6

Medical mishaps

I know that God won't give me more trouble than
I can handle . . . but I sometimes wish he wouldn't
trust me so much.
— Mother Teresa

Almost immediately after I was settled in my new room (a private room!) in the plastics ward, I was sent for a CAT scan. It was dinnertime and there were no hospital aides available to transport me. That was left to my exhausted eighty-year-old mother who was coping now without my sisters. We arrived on time for the appointment, but were kept waiting for so long that eventually the other patient, having pity at the sight of me, offered to let me in ahead of him. I was amazed at how exhausting it was just to sit upright in a wheelchair for all that time.

The scan was meant to be taken with me in a position

I couldn't manage. Because of external metal rods screwed through the skin of my leg and tightened by wing nuts to hold my broken bone together, I was forced instead into a contorted position with my head, which had so recently undergone twelve-hour surgery, tilted at an extreme angle. It was all they could do, given how much of me was broken, but it was my first indication that a medical system that is divided into specialty areas is sometimes poorly equipped to deal with more than one part of the patient at a time. A compartmentalised medical system cannot respond to a patient in any way other than by dividing individuals into categories according to symptom and dealing with them accordingly, like a broken machine. By the time the CAT scans were complete and I returned to my room, the dinner hour was over and my untouched meal tray had been removed from my bedside.

I no longer had my own nurse, as I had had in intensive care, but I never lacked attention. In fact, there were many times that I wished I had less attention. Compared to being in intensive care, life in the ward was a whirlwind of activity. Medical staff in different specialty areas, none of whom seemed to be coordinating with the others, arrived to take me for X-rays, for lab work, and for consultations with surgeons specialising in: ophthalmology, dentistry, audiology, orthopaedics, plastic surgery . . .

Within each specialty were specialists! One eye doctor saw me about pressure behind my eye and double vision. Another saw me for a torn tear duct, although both problems existed simultaneously. Even the surgical team assigned to me had two rather than one senior surgeon and two registrars. I was whisked away from meals, from friends who had travelled an hour to visit me, from much-needed naps and even once had two hospital aides competing to take me to different departments at the same time. It was exhausting. More than once I was left waiting alone in my wheelchair or bed in the hospital corridor after an appointment for long periods because aides were otherwise occupied.

Within my first few days in the ward, three medical mishaps in a row worked to undermine my newly found confidence and optimism. The first day I was taken into a room to have a patch of skin removed from my thigh for a graft. To my horror I felt a sharp pain as a scalpel cut into my flesh. I screamed and was quickly administered more anaesthetic and the job finished before I was sent, stunned, back to my room. I had already been through so much that I easily let the incident go. Mistakes happen and too much had been done to save my life to focus on this.

In the night, lying in the same position on my back with a plastic-covered mattress beneath my sheets, I was sweating and itched horribly. I asked a night nurse if she couldn't please wipe my back with a cool sponge. She refused. 'There aren't enough of us here to be giving you a bath at night. You'll have to wait until morning like the others.' The itching continued throughout the following day, even after my bath. A different nurse was on that night, so I risked asking again for some relief. She was good enough to agree to a cool sponge bath, but noticed something amiss and called the house surgeon, who quickly diagnosed that I had scabies burrowing into my back. A few phone calls revealed that a young boy had come into the intensive care unit with scabies while I was there. I had been infected with scabies in the intensive care unit, of all places. Again, I was stunned, yet the solution was easy and I was so relieved to stop itching that gratitude quickly overcame my dismay.

The next day (or possibly the one after?) I had my first shower. It was the first time that I was able to bathe myself — in private. I was transferred by two nurses into a special wheelchair that had a toilet seat rather than a regular seat. The nurse helped to undress me then left me alone in the shower stall with a hand-held nozzle, to take however much time I wanted to indulge in the exquisite sensation of warm water striking my skin like thousands of tiny fingers. Had I been in a muddy trench for a month, it could not have been a more delicious experience — especially to return to freshly changed sheets and my beautiful new nightgown.

So I was not at all apprehensive when sometime later a nurse I knew came in with a tall male student nurse to transfer me from my bed into a chair. She described exactly how they were going to make the transfer, presumably for his instruction as well as my own. She would support my left leg, which was the most obviously damaged with the metal fixators holding it together, and he would support me with my right arm around his neck and his left arm around my waist as I placed my weight onto my right leg. She was a nurse. She must do this all the time. So, naturally, I followed her instruction to the letter, even though my right leg, which was held together with an internal, rather than external, rod was also badly fractured. As soon as I stood on my right leg, I collapsed in excruciating pain. The student nurse jerked upright to his full six-foot-something height and

I felt a searing pain rip through my right shoulder and arm — the only limb not already damaged! It hurt to breathe and the following day X-rays showed broken ribs on my right side. I never saw the student nurse again and to this day my shoulder has never healed. I am told that one day I will need a complete shoulder replacement.

I was transferred to the orthopaedic ward soon after that incident for the remainder of my hospital stay. No one ever offered an apology. The gap between my needs and my confidence in my caregivers became a chasm I could never again cross. Although there were many fine doctors and nurses looking after me, I was constantly on guard against further oversights and injuries.

I found out much later when reading my hospital file, that during his operation, my plastic surgeon had noted that the soft tissue in the still open wound of my left leg appeared 'quite dirty'. It had been at least ten days since the orthopaedic registrar had fitted an internal metal rod through the length of my tibia to stabilise my fractures immediately following the accident. A different orthopaedic registrar was on duty when my plastic surgery was being performed. She was called in and removed the metal rod, replacing it with an external fixator, a device made up of six bolts passing through my skin into my bone and attached to external rods with nuts and bolts holding it all in place. I was to live with that fixator for the next ten months. Although the original stabilisation was, according to my records, 'anatomically correct', the fixator left my lower leg rotated at a permanent angle to my knee and ankle.

Given the circumstances of the accident there would have

been risk of infection to the bone and the possible eventual loss of my leg. One has to wonder, was I 'lucky'? It was a question I asked myself many times during my recovery and which I rarely had the generosity of spirit to answer with a clear 'Yes!' No matter how many people told me that I should consider myself lucky, I found it difficult at the time to consider my glass half full rather than half empty.

7

Life on the ward

I'm in an acute orthopaedic ward where the average age is over eighty. Sometimes it is literally a madhouse in here. I catch myself wavering between self-pity, anger, revulsion and feelings of compassion, humour and peace. Sometimes I feel I am going crazy myself.

I tried to see the move to the orthopaedic ward as a step forward in my recovery, though I found it hard to leave the room that had already come to feel like my new 'home'. When you're bedridden it's easy to become jealously possessive of the small space that you do have control over. In the plastics ward it was an entire room that people entered only to visit or care for me. It was 'my space'. It had my name on the door.

In the orthopaedic ward, 'my space' was reduced to one of four curtained-off beds in a room that housed mostly elderly women patients, some suffering dementia as well as broken hips. I was to spend the next three months living in close proximity with a series of strangers, some of whom didn't know where they were or why. We would share intimacies sometimes not shared even by close family members simply by virtue of being bedridden in the same small space. We cleared our bowels or bladders with only a curtain for privacy even when others' visitors were present. Sometimes I sat in excruciating pain and humiliation for as long as a half-hour, not wanting to let the strangers on the other side of my curtain hear me cry, as I waited for someone to answer my bell and remove my bedpan. We ate together, listened to each other snoring at night or to each other's private conversations with visitors in the day. Sometimes we even listened to each other's conflicting radio or television stations. And on a few rare but distressing occasions I had to keep myself from lashing out at the demented ravings of frightened and disoriented old women whose bodies lay only feet from my bed but whose minds were far away from the scene I couldn't escape.

I remember in particular one elderly woman who often fell into demented and disoriented pantomimes of wherever it was that her mind had taken her, but whose stroppy and independent spirit shone through. I liked her! At first 'Millie' kicked off her sheets, exposing her genitals to whoever happened to pass in the hallway as she furiously tugged at her catheter. That got the nurses' attention! They quickly covered her up, clucking, 'Shame on you!' as if this poor woman had any idea of anything other than the fact that something was poking out from between her legs!

One day after perhaps an hour of sitting in her bed across the room from me focused on repeating the same shovelling motion, she started to try to climb out of her bed. I buzzed the nurse furiously as I tried to get Millie's attention to prevent her from falling out of bed.

'Millie, no! No! You can't get up! You'll hurt yourself!' I called to her from across the room.

She looked at me as though I was mad. 'I've been gardening all day,' she patiently explained. 'I'm tired and I want to go in the house.'

'No! Millie, you're in a hospital. You're sick. You can't walk! Neither can I!'

I will never forget the look she gave me, almost pitying, as she replied with a shrug, 'If that's the way you see it!'

Luckily a nurse came in and pulled the restraining bars in place. I envied her then — happily working away in her garden, unaware of her limits, while I was stuck in a hospital bed only a few feet away.

Another elderly patient who was with us only a short time, was trapped in a nightmare of perpetual fear, screaming at all hours of day or night for help. When nurses approached her she whimpered and begged like a little girl expecting a beating, although the nurses were kind and reassuring. A woman elsewhere in the orthopaedic ward kept calling out a man's name pleadingly. 'John! John!' A nurse confided to me that this was not the name of her husband, who visited regularly but whom she didn't recognise. I sometimes felt like Jack Nicholson in *One Flew Over The Cuckoo's Nest*. What was *I* doing here?

Then 'Laura' came. She was a breath of fresh air. At

eighty-five she had a seventy-eight-year-old husband that she referred to as her 'toy boy'. She was in for a hip replacement, her second. Just as with the first hip replacement the previous year, her surgery fell on her birthday. With a full voice she sang 'Happy Birthday' to herself and the staff joined in. She was like a visiting hostess, entertaining all of us and making us smile. But after her surgery she found it difficult to hold food down. I noticed that she ate very little. When the doctor arrived on his weekly ward rounds he asked her if she had been up to practise walking.

'I'm having trouble eating, doctor,' she replied.

'You've got to eat to get better!' he cheerfully told her. 'Now let's get you up and walking.'

I listened to Laura coughing and struggling for breath at night and told a nurse of my concerns.

'She did the same thing last year,' the nurse replied.

I didn't understand. Did she think Laura was misbehaving? The following week when her surgeon arrived again for ward rounds, I expressed my concerns to him.

'I'm really worried about her.' (Always the 'helper'!) 'She's not eating and she's coughing all night.' Laura explained that it was difficult to hold food down.

'You have to make a real effort to eat,' the doctor reminded her, 'and you have to move to keep your lungs clear. You need to practise walking every day.'

Laura got worse. She was vomiting now as well as coughing. I thought she was going to die. Once, when she vomited all over herself, I called a nurse to help her. But the nurse didn't have time to clean her up just then. Laura sat slumped in her wheelchair covered in vomit for more than

51

an hour as I sat helplessly across from her, unable to get out of bed. Eventually her son, a doctor, arrived from Canada. An oxygen tank was brought in and Laura was taken away for X-rays. But she still didn't eat. And she never sang any more. One day they took her away to Waitakere Hospital, a convalescent home. Before she left she told me that she didn't think she'd be going home again. She'd come in singing and was wheeled away with little will to live. Or so it seemed to me. After she left I reached for my mascot, a small, blue plastic boxing kangaroo with bright pink gloves that I kept on my bedside table. I wound the kangaroo up and watched as it fought valiantly, hopping across the table and punching at the air. Then I wound it up again. And again. It was my personal reminder to keep on fighting to get better and to never give up!

8

Is anybody listening?

*The greatest gift you can give another is the purity
of your attention.*
— Richard Moss

I'd been told by one of the registrars that I was being
moved from plastics to the orthopaedics ward so that I
could have 'daily, rigorous physiotherapy'. So much of who I
felt myself to be I had previously expressed physically. I had
always considered myself strong, vital, outdoorsy, and fairly
attractive, with a tight and youthful body. Physiotherapy
would be a welcome challenge to reclaim all of that. I
couldn't wait!

So, when the physiotherapist came to see me shortly
after I arrived, I sat up like an eager student, ready to impress
my teacher. I greeted her excitedly. When could we start? She
pulled back the sheets, took one look at the external metal

rods holding the splintered bones of my left tibia in place, threw the sheet back over me and shook her head.

'Not much we can do here, I'm afraid,' she announced and started to walk away.

'Hang on a second!' I called after her. 'What do you mean? I'm ready! There must be something I can do!' I was devastated. Her gruff manner softened and she returned to my side.

'You can't bend this knee for at least six weeks and you can't go into a pool with external rods,' she explained. 'You have to give the bones time to heal.'

'But what *can* I do?' I insisted. I couldn't just lie there passively for six more weeks watching my muscles waste away. She gave me some basic stomach tightening exercises that I could do lying in place and permission to do exercises for my wrist that I'd told her hurt too much to even hold a cup of tea. Then she went away on vacation, leaving me to wait it out. I've never been good at waiting. Several times a day I did my workout, squeezing my buttocks, arching my back and doing tummy crunches. To this day I have tight abdominal and lower back muscles.

As much as I didn't like it, a lot of my day was spent waiting. Waiting to be lifted into my special wheelchair for a shower in the morning, waiting for the distraction of meals, waiting (sometimes endlessly) for my buzzer to be answered, for visitors to arrive and, most eagerly, waiting for the weekly ward rounds where one or both of the orthopaedic surgeons and registrars came with medical students to review my progress. Although I was only one of possibly fifty or more patients seen by the team over the course of the morning, this few minutes was the part of my week that I anticipated most eagerly. Throughout the week I looked forward to telling the doctors of important symptoms I noticed and asking the questions that might help me to understand what was happening — and likely to happen — to me. I awaited understanding, hope and reassurance. It was my one opportunity to actually be involved in my treatment and I was desperate for that involvement.

Sometimes one or other registrar came independently of the ward rounds and I would discuss my questions or concerns with them. In my inflated sense of what occurred behind the scenes, I imagined that whatever I discussed with any member of the team was noted in my chart and discussed by the rest of the team. I complained repeatedly to nurses, to the registrars, and to the physiotherapist about the pain in my wrist and my inability to use it to lift so much as a cup of tea or lift the cover off my dinner plate. My complaints were largely ignored with comments like, 'Of course it hurts, your arm was broken,' and, 'Just use the other hand.' Both the physiotherapist and one of the registrars said it was fine to do exercises to keep my wrist flexible. No one referred to my chart or made notes of my complaints.

The stiffer and more useless my wrist became, the more I gritted my teeth and did wrist flexes to keep it mobile. It wasn't until ten weeks after the accident, when I was about to have an operation to graft more bone on to my tibia so that I could finally walk with the help of crutches, that anyone took notice of my complaints. When he announced the upcoming surgery to me during the ward rounds, I asked the surgeon how I could possibly bear my weight on a crutch if I couldn't even hold a cup of tea in that hand. He was unaware that there was any problem. Everyone there for the ward rounds, except for the medical students, had heard it before. The team left and the surgeon came back to my bedside alone sometime later to explain that a broken bone in my wrist was 'somehow overlooked'. It was the first and only time that I yelled at a surgeon. It was *I* that was overlooked! It was clearly stated in the radiology report of the X-rays taken on the day of the accident that the scaphoid bone of my left wrist was broken. And, following my initial surgery, it was again reported that X-rays showed my scaphoid bone was still broken! Had anyone taken my complaints seriously this wouldn't have happened. I had waited so long to stand on my own two feet again and now would have to wait again for attempts to reconnect my scaphoid bone before I could even attempt to bear weight using my forearm rather than my wrist and a special crutch.

Of this incident I confess I remain bitter. We are none of us infallible. Mistakes happen. But there is constant danger to the wellbeing of patients (not to mention the finances of the hospital) in assuming that surgeons are an exception to this rule. Every staff member on that ward who heard my complaints and assumed that the doctor knew better than I whether or not there was a genuine problem, contributed to the pain I endured unnecessarily, to the ten weeks that my wrist remained broken, to the following five months that my wrist remained in a cast, leaving me physically dependent, and to the thousands of dollars it cost the public health system for the three additional operations it took to eventually correct the problem. Had I had the energy or inclination to sue for medical malpractice through the government accident insurance agency, it might have cost the hospital much more than that.

Double-checking is not a sign of weakness. Being a patient is not a sign of stupidity. And being busy is not an excuse. In the end, a lot more time and money was spent on correcting this problem than it would have taken to follow up on my repeated complaints. To listen!

People often wonder why I feel bitter about this particular experience and less so about the nurse-inflicted injury to my shoulder that debilitates me still. Or even to the accident itself. It's true that it was the drunk driver who put me in the hospital in the first place, and that the many doctors and nurses who performed my initial surgeries and tended to me in intensive care saved both my life and my leg. I have a great deal to be grateful to them for. But both the accident and the injury to my shoulder were unintended acts of carelessness. There was nothing at all personal or deliberate about either. The doctors, nurses and the physiotherapist who heard my complaints about my wrist, long after the initial crisis had passed, repeatedly chose to discount and invalidate my experience. In doing so, they added to my sense of invisibility and helplessness when what I needed, possibly more than any other thing at that point, was to have myself, my true experience, reflected back at me and validated. With all of the external evidence of who I was so dramatically altered, it was crucial that my internal experience not be denied. Without that reflection from the world around me, I was lost.

I felt I had lost my identity. Kathy Torpie had been replaced by patient #BHK3105. So I clung tenaciously to my identity with medical staff, who (understandably) found it difficult to remember so many patients' names. I told every new nurse as nicely as I could that my name was Kathy. Not 'Love' or even 'Mrs Torpie'. (I'm single.) When I was being referred to by doctors in my own presence as 'she' or 'the patient', I'd remind both them and myself, 'I'm Kathy. It's written on the card above my bed.' I hung on to that like a mantra. 'I'm Kathy.' Though the reflection in the mirror offered no reassurance that that was so. Friends who visited seemed to see only Kathy and with gratitude I tried to be her. But the person on the inside began to doubt that the Kathy who they had come to visit still existed.

9

Why me?

Some people think that everything happens for a reason. I prefer to think that every experience is an opportunity to learn or, perhaps, to remember some reality outside of our current construction of how things are. How we choose to interpret and respond to that opportunity can literally change the world as we experience it.

After several weeks of asking the proverbial 'Why me?', I was struck by the answer . . . 'Shit happens.' It was as profound — and unwelcome — an answer as I could have imagined, because I was hit with the simple truth of it. 'Shit' does indeed happen. But, more than that, life happens, and there is no getting out of its way without dying. While life is happening we don't even notice most of the time. We notice only the 'shit' — the accidents, disappointments and losses that are an inevitable part of life. That's why we make up clichés about them. But what of the rest of life? What of all the things that are happening around us and within us and between us that we don't notice unless they're unusually bad or unusually good? 'Shit happens.' It was so simple and so true that it made me laugh.

Helplessness is probably the most unpalatable of all human emotions. We will go to almost any length to avoid experiencing it. Rape and abuse victims, accident victims, parents helpless to save their children, will often blame themselves for not having been able to prevent the losses they now face rather than accept the fact of their helplessness. 'If only . . .', 'I should (shouldn't) have . . .', 'I wish I had . . .' Searching for what they might have done differently rather than allowing the devastating knowledge that there was absolutely nothing they could have done to prevent what happened, that the world is not necessarily a safe place after all, that disaster is often arbitrary, and that all we so naively take for granted is not entirely within our control. No matter what we lose, the loss of this innocence can be the most devastating and enduring loss of all.

I knew an instant before the accident that there was nothing I could do to prevent it, though my mind screamed for some way out. Of course I went through all of the 'if onlys' after the fact. If only I had left the restaurant a few minutes earlier or later. If only I had stayed home that night. If only . . . But there was nothing I could have done! Later, when my breathing tube dislodged from my throat or when my bowels released against my will or even when my meal tray was left out of my reach and no one answered my call button, my sense of helplessness was reinforced. There was nothing I could do!

Shortly after I was moved into the orthopaedic ward, an acquaintance from Muriwai with New Age leanings came to visit. There I lay with metal rods drilled into my leg, with my misshapen face and withering limbs. The first thing she said, after taking in the pitiful picture of what I looked like, was, 'Why do you think you created this in your life?' Under the circumstances it seemed an absurdly insensitive thing to say. But on some level I understood that, like the rest of us, she was looking for some rationale that would deny the sometimes random nature of life and the helplessness that any one of us might experience. She was simply looking for some reassuring explanation for suffering. Something to protect her from the terrible knowledge that this could just as easily have happened to her. It was safer to reason that if we are the creators of our own misfortune, then we have the power to be completely free of any misfortune. That we can live in perfect health, in full prosperity, in relationships unblemished by conflict, if only we choose to. I, apparently, had chosen to have a head-on collision instead.

'I didn't create this,' I replied through my wired teeth. 'Oneness did. The universe did. Whatever you want to call it. We all created this together. Life is constantly creating opportunities to respond to it, some more dramatic than others. This accident had a deep impact not only on me, but on my family and friends, on the driver of the other car and on his family and friends, and on the medical staff. And the people in their lives were affected by the impact it had on them. There are lessons to learn from this for all of us.'

'Why me?' I had asked it of myself. 'Why did this thing happen to me? Why now? Why, when I was living life so authentically, so gently, when I finally felt like I'd found a place to call "home"? Why?' . . . 'Why not?' came the reply from some place deep within, a voice that until now had been silent. 'You can't control life. You can only respond to it.' The unyielding control freak in me was confronted with the slow realisation that no matter how carefully I respond, I can't control the outcome of my response. That there are no 'right' answers to life's problems. That life is just a random set of experiences and a chosen set of responses to those experiences. Each response stimulates a new experience. It's like a cosmic game of pinball. From the distance it's fascinating. It's keeping the distance while staying in the game that's the challenge.

After I finally began to come to grips with that unpalatable truth — and even saw some humour in it — I started asking different questions. Why, for example, if my entire face was crushed and both eye sockets shattered, can I still see? Why, if my body was so badly broken, was my spine uninjured? Why was I still alive? I realised that the only way that I could 'create my reality' was by choosing how I interpret it.

I'm alive, I decided, for no other reason than to experience life and to respond to it with awareness. Not to fight it. Not to conquer it like a mountain, as I always had, but to flow with it like a river — with the rapids, the still water and the back eddies that seem to have no escape, but always do. Although I couldn't control the outcome of my responses to what life put in my path, I could, with every conscious or unconscious choice I made, have an impact on the overall harmony or disharmony of life itself. I still had my eyes and all my other sense organs to help me experience life and respond with awareness. As long as my eyes were open, sight might be happening. But unless I actually looked, unless I paid attention, I couldn't really see what was there, couldn't truly experience life or respond to it fully.

Without some sense of predictability or control over events that shaped my life (or even assured its continuation), I no longer knew what to be guided by. I could no longer pretend to myself that if I was good enough, smart enough, powerful enough, that if I just got it 'right' I could keep myself safe and shape my own destiny. If there was no 'right' way, no answer, if life didn't actually make sense as I'd always believed, if it wasn't simply a matter of finding the right solutions to life's problems, if in fact life was simply a process to be experienced and responded to and I didn't exist except as part of an infinite set of relationships with the rest of life . . . The implications were overwhelming and more than a little threatening to my previously well-defended ego. I had lost not only my physical sense of myself — my vitality, mobility and appearance — but with it my way of relating to the world around me. I'd lost everything I ever held to be 'real', everything that who and how I am in the world had previously been based on. I had no idea how I could continue to function in the world with any authenticity without that to guide me.

For much of my life — as a student, as a psychologist, and as a woman — I met life with the childish belief that I had to earn my status in the world. Always striving to do or be better. I tried to earn a special place in my father's eyes by working for straight 'As'. Every 'B' was seen as a failure and evidence that I needed to improve. I often worked overtime or into the night to improve my clinical work and, as a woman, I felt I needed to prove my independence so that any relationship with a man would be on an equal footing. Now I was bitterly disappointed that I wasn't responding as I believed one who had a close call with death should respond — with saintly humility, compassion and joy.

Self-improvement groups make their fortunes from this human drive to be more . . . more assertive, more successful, more enlightened . . . The list is endless. At one of these groups, a woman's psychodrama group that I attended many years ago, we were all asked to stand in a line that ran diagonally from one end of the room to the other. We were to position ourselves relative to the others according to where we felt we were in terms of whatever issues we had come to the group with. Then we were to physically change our positions — to move along the line to where we each felt we stood now. The group leader interviewed each of us asking where we were at the beginning of the group ten weeks earlier and where we stood now. Then with some dramatic flair, she pointed to the end of the line. To the point that represented 100 per cent. She asked each woman in turn what she needed to do to get from here to there. 'I need to be more assertive', 'I need to believe in myself more', 'I need to go back to school' came the replies. When she came to me and my attention was directed (once again) to the magic 100 per cent, something in me rebelled. 'I'm sick and tired of 100 per cent!' I railed. 'Eighty-five per cent is just fine with me!' That's how I felt now. Tired of a self-imposed struggle to be

100 per cent, to be perfect. It was this drive for perfection that left me so often feeling exhausted and so rarely fully satisfied.

I knew that I'd been given the opportunity to embark on a rite of passage, to mature into a much more substantial and meaningful way of living, but that I was still stuck at the point of entry. I wanted to be more accepting of the shadow side of my humanity — my needs, my fears, my anger, my games — and more accepting of the human inadequacies of others. I wanted to break my addiction to being 'right' wherever that made others 'wrong'. But I could get so easily lost in my emotions, in satisfying my ego, that I doubted I would ever make the passage to spiritual 'adulthood'. Being compassionate didn't feel as powerful as being angry, or as satisfying to my ego as being right, or as safe as being in control. Yet, in that brief moment in the intensive care unit when I hung between life and death and experienced a tenderness and compassion for the human experience unlike anything I had ever felt before, I felt more at peace and at home than I ever had with any of those other feelings.

It seemed impossible to actually live my life as 'One' with the divine, even though I'd been given the opportunity to see that that's who I was when the curtain came down on this performance called life. Ever since Adam and Eve bit into that damn apple, human beings have struggled to reconcile the tension between good and evil, right and wrong, independence and dependence . . . and all of the opposing forces that are the very nature of the physical world that we're born into. In that world 'shit' does indeed happen. And when it does, it presents us with rich compost in which life continues to grow and renew. Nature doesn't try to eliminate the 'bad'. Only humanity does that, in its desperate struggle to find the way back to Eden. Nature uses the 'shit' we so desperately want to eliminate, in an ever-continuing process of seeking balance between the opposing forces that shape both our world and our psyches.

I had decided to carry on living and with that decision came the fact that I would continue to be as humanly fallible as anyone else. Being perfect wasn't the point. But learning to forgive the imperfect just might be.

10

Losing face

It is such an ugly face that I now wear. But more people have told me lately how 'beautiful' I am than I've ever been told before. Did I hide behind my face when it was more attractive because I feared that some of the ugliness of the person behind the face might be discovered? It turns out that there is more beauty and ugliness behind this face than I ever let myself imagine.

Sometimes the greatest pain associated with losing a loved one is the knowledge that you will never see that person again. It takes a while before you stop half expecting to see that person turn the corner or walk in the door. Sometimes a photo, a child's favourite toy, a piece of music, or a familiar scent may elicit a memory so strong that the loss momentarily ceases to exist. It took years before I could accept that I would never see my own face again. In the hospital I kept a photo of my former self by my bedside and several times a day looked into a mirror expecting to see 'me'. Instead, always, again and again, I was greeted by the bewildered, flattened gaze of a stranger. The pain of seeing this stranger's face when some crazy hope made me half expect to see my own familiar reflection was at times so physically stunning that it took my breath away.

In the very beginning, when I was first made aware that I had no face, no facial features, it didn't seem all that important. I knew beyond any shadow of a doubt that I was more than a mere body. I felt so close to God and the infinite in my critical condition that I was fairly indifferent to my appearance (though my mother is convinced to this day that it was the drugs). I'm told that on the second day after the accident I indicated that I wanted to communicate in writing with my one good arm and with some difficulty I wrote: 'Lost my face. Not my spirit.' I wanted to reassure horrified friends and family that it wasn't so tragic. I still have that note, written in an awkward scrawl resembling that of a four-year-old. But as time went on and the expansiveness I felt in the face of death was replaced with the contracted passivity of my life as a patient, I lost my spirit and my ego took over. Eventually I became obsessed with reclaiming my face. Without it I felt homeless.

Each of us has a 'face' that we present to the world, a face that identifies and distinguishes us from others. This face is both source and symptom of our separateness. The physical face that we are born with is only part of the image we project onto the world. The way we dress, the way we look and act, our jobs and social roles are all part of our identity or 'face'.

It includes all of the ways in which we express ourselves — show our intellect or humour — qualities we want to be recognised for. We hide the unacceptable, 'shadow' side of ourselves behind the faces we wear. We cling to this face because it is our own and because it is what differentiates us as unique individuals in the world. Most of us come to believe so strongly in the image that we have perfected over a lifetime, that we think it's who we actually are! Ask anyone 'Who are you?' and the vast majority will respond with their name, their job, their marital status or family role, their nationality, perhaps their age and sex. But, who are we beyond that? Who are we really?

> *Illness causes questions: Who are you when you stop doing? When you cannot be productive or are no longer indispensable to others? When you can no longer go on as before because you are sick, when you lose status? Who are you when you can't be a caretaker or a boss or do your job, whatever that might be?*
> — Dr Jean Shinoda Bolen, *Close to the Bone*

At some level we are all terrified of 'losing face' — of being stripped naked of our identity or status and, in many cases of our hiding places. When I woke in intensive care I had not only no identifiable physical face, but no means whatsoever of projecting my personality. In the months that followed I was reduced to the role and status of patient. I had little means of distinguishing myself from other patients other than by symptom. I was 'the multi-trauma'. Patient #BHK3105.

I followed the same routines, ate the same food, went to bed and woke up at the same time as all the strangers that filled the other hospital beds. I felt that I had lost not only my physical face, but my entire identity. Yet in that one moment when I was closest to death, I had discovered another 'identity' that lay hidden behind the face I had lost. It was the face of divinity that we all so cleverly disguise with our individual and separate identities. It was beautiful beyond anything I could have imagined and in no way mine alone. The separateness, that is so much a part of the human condition and so often a cause of deep suffering, was no more than a single divine source giving birth to all of the unlimited possible expressions of itself. Every individual was just another face of God! I remember the profound gratitude I felt at the time to actually know that that is who and what I really am. But I kept forgetting. How does one keep the infinite in perspective in this world of separate egos?

In the years since the accident I have come to know both the hateful bitterness and the loving compassion that exist behind the faces I wear in the world. No face is adequate to express the totality of who we are or even how we feel at any moment. In showing only part of who I am, the rest remains hidden, even from myself. Yet human perception is so narrow that we need to be presented with a face, an image, a partial reflection of the true self (and a mask to hide disowned parts of the self). Getting to know a person is a matter of seeing the repertoire of faces that person presents. It is like getting to know the characters on your favourite television show without ever getting to know the actors. (Real actors know that the emotions and qualities of the characters they play are all contained within themselves — no matter how different that character may be from the way that the actor presents him or herself in daily life.)

I watched myself respond to the indignities of patient life with angry and defensive behaviour. Gone was the divinity! It seemed imperative to my very survival that I assert myself and my personal rights at every opportunity. I recall especially one incident when an agency nurse filling in to look after the post-operative patient in the bed next to mine unplugged the CPM machine that mobilised my damaged knee by degrees. I asked her not to do that.

Shocked at my assertion she marched crisply over to my bed and announced, 'Perhaps I should introduce myself. I am sister [so and so], an agency nurse here to look after this patient. You have a plug on your own side.'

'My Walkman is plugged in there,' I explained.

'Oh, now wouldn't that be a great loss,' she countered as she began to march away.

Something inside me snapped. 'Perhaps I should introduce *myself*,' I called out to her receding back.

'I am Kathy Torpie and I am a patient. I live here! This six-by-four-foot space is my world and the Walkman is my one and only personal pleasure. I can't read, move or watch television. Please plug it back in. There is an empty space with a plug for your patient over there!'

There was stunned silence before the nurse turned on her heels and huffed her way out of the room. I knew I wasn't making friends with the staff by refusing a passive, obedient role. I was fiercely protective of what little independence or personal comfort I had. I knew I needed that to survive.

Everyone is concerned with the medical problem, not with the psyche: the message a patient gets is to keep your fears to yourself and put on a good face; be a good girl or act like a man, and do what the doctor says. You are not to be angry. You are not to question authority. You are now in the underworld of your fears but are not to mention it. If you are angry or self-pitying, if you become emotional, if you want doctors or nurses to pay attention to your feelings, you are being a problem. Attending to emotions takes time and when there is just so much time to do hospital rounds, or so much time allotted to see each patient, a patient or a relative who needs or wants reassurance or further explanations is often seen as demanding or even as requiring a psychiatric consultation.

— Dr Jean Shinoda Bolen, *Close To The Bone*

I was visited later by a psychologist who explained that if I upset staff they would not want to work with me and that I should try to be a better 'team player'.

'One of the most important things I have learned from this experience,' I replied, 'is the absolute need to be authentic if I am to recover.' I was beginning to realise the enormous disabling cost of trying, always, to please, to impress, to entertain . . . to earn care.

'Couldn't you be just a little less authentic?' he replied.

On another occasion a nurse aide decided to tidy the stand next to my bed while I showered. She put all of my personal things neatly away . . . where I couldn't reach them.

When I asked her (nicely) to please put them back within my reach, she too was offended. She said my night stand was too messy. It was as if my caregivers and I were actually on opposing teams!

There wasn't much I could do in a hospital bed for four months other than observe what went on around me and within me. And, as a psychologist, that's exactly what I did. The 'faces', as I saw them, of many of the people that I depended on were officious, distant, controlling and often arrogant. I was seeing them through the eyes of a frightened, exhausted, vulnerable patient. I was needy. I needed gentle, compassionate care, respect, acknowledgement of my person and inclusion in my treatment.

After a while I began to recognise that the individuals behind those faces had needs of their own. Overworked, often understaffed, and surrounded daily by human suffering, doctors and nurses nonetheless need to feel competent in their work. To protect themselves from the suffering and loss that surrounded them, I was certain that some created emotional distance by objectifying patients. Those who apparently most needed to feel helpful were the ones who tended to take over or to discount patient concerns with empty reassurances. But the more they took charge without including me, the more helpless I felt. I saw that we were all caught in the same pressure cooker with conflicting personal needs interfering with our mutual goal — the patient's recovery.

Budget cuts and time pressures turned patient 'contact' into patient 'load', which in turn fostered hierarchical rather than collaborative relationships between patient and staff and passive rather than active involvement by patients in their recovery. While I knew this, I knew too that the very spirit that gave the life they had saved meaning was being annihilated by my objectification as a patient. The endless struggle to protect myself — and my spirit — from passive objectivity depleted the resources I needed for recovery and alienated those I depended on. The face that they saw was that of a 'difficult patient'.

Anyone who has experienced a dramatic identity crisis knows what I'm talking about. Sudden divorce, redundancy at work, having your first baby or having the last child leave home, can all lead one to wonder, 'Who am I without the familiar roles or qualities I once defined myself by? Who am I really?'

In the course of my recovery, my periods stopped and I entered menopause. Another identifying quality gone! I lost my emotional as well as physical 'home' and noticed with horror when my concentration and memory began to slip. Later, as friends struggled with the emotional and physical changes brought about by their own menopausal experience, they began to better understand the alienation I experienced from my altered body image following the accident — though mine occurred in an instant rather than over a span of years.

None of us is without loss in our lives. And none without altered body image, though luckily most experience this slowly. All of us can look at a photo of ourselves as small children with the realisation that, although the reflection in the mirror today may be a far cry from the child's face, and our experience of the world as different as the faces we wore then and now, there is a common thread that is 'me'. Sometimes the entire fabric of our lives needs to be torn away before we can begin to unravel that thread.

11

Origins of the mask

Most people love you for who you pretend to be . . . To keep their love, you keep pretending-performing. You get to love your pretense . . . It's true, we're locked in an image, an act. And the sad thing is, people get so used to their image... they grow attached to their masks. They love their chains. They forget all about who they really are. And, if you try to remind them, they hate you for it. They feel like you are trying to steal their most precious possession.

— James Douglas Morrison, lead singer of The Doors

Even though we biologically inherit a predisposition towards certain characteristics, from eye colour to temperament to general IQ, much of who we appear to be — to others and to ourselves — is learned from our early interaction with others. We are all taught, both directly and indirectly, the need to present an acceptable face to the world and to hide the unacceptable from view. None of us is immune to this process, though some are more profoundly affected than others.

When we are born we have no awareness of existing separately from the world around us. For the first several weeks of life there is no distinction between self and other. There is no 'me' and no 'you'. For that matter, we come into the world with no awareness of anything other than the present moment. We can remember no past nor project any future. It is ironic that many spiritual masters spend a lifetime engaged in various practices to re-create that same sense of oneness and of living in the moment. You might say that we are all born 'enlightened' and that we forget oneness rather than learn that we have a separate identity. But I digress . . .

Differentiation, the beginning of the process of separation and individuation, doesn't begin until about the fourth or fifth month of life. We become aware that there is a separate 'me' as well as all that is 'not me'. We are neither the pain nor the gratification that we experience, but we experience both in relation to something outside of ourselves. The fact is that we are dependent and vulnerable but we don't yet know the implications of that. We haven't yet learned the art of relating as a separate individual. That takes practice. Once we can crawl and eventually can walk, we are free to explore more of our immediate world. We return frequently to check that 'mother' is within reach, but learn that there are other significant people in our lives. We learn to relate to other toddlers and adults, and in the process, learn to judge their behaviour and to work out how they judge ours.

By about the third year of life we have moved from the simple awareness that separation exists, to developing a sense of who that separate individual is. The ego, the unique sense of self in relation to the world we know, has by then begun the lifelong phase of self-definition. But along the way we also have to learn who it is acceptable for us to be in order to meet the expectations of others. We learn to create a social 'face' for the world to see. For many, that acceptable social face can keep the rest of who we are hidden, even from ourselves.

Whenever my family members reminisced about our early childhoods, my mother would shake her head at what a 'spoiled child' I was. I was one of four children under the age of six in post-war America. My next-door neighbours were an elderly Jewish couple with lots of time on their hands. And a bowl of candies on their coffee table! I visited often. I entertained and charmed them and was rewarded with the attention I craved as well as a piece of candy when I left. Did they 'spoil' me? I suppose that for a mother of four preschoolers who couldn't possibly give me that kind of attention, they did. But I managed to learn that, except perhaps for an overtired mother, a bit of charm and dramatic flair — being funny and entertaining — could make a lonely child the focus of positive attention. When I reached fourth grade my best friend and I put on a lunchtime performance for the entire school. Fifteen years later, as a teacher, I was still a bit of a ham. And I was still lonely. Everyone loved my character, but nobody really knew who I was off-stage.

In high school I was in advanced classes one or two years ahead of many of my peers. I loved maths and science but I hated the 'square' (read geek) image that went with it. So I ratted my hair and smoked cigarettes in the girls' room and spoke with a practised New York accent. I did the best I could to appear tough. But my homework was always in on time and the only ones who seemed to believe the bad-girl image I tried to create for myself were my parents!

Then a miracle happened. I felt unsatisfied enough to realise that 'fitting in' wasn't worth the price. I was a third-year teacher by then and popular with my students. I was working in a prestige community and about to receive tenure when I quit at the end of the school year because I wanted to do something for me, something selfish, indulgent, irresponsible. I became a ski-bum. I waited tables. I made and sold jewellery. And I skied every day! It was the first time in my life that I stepped completely outside of the expectation — that I had by now made my own — that I excel, that I be popular and that I achieve. Little did I realise that my need to excel was so ingrained that I turned my self-indulgent independent lifestyle into an art form. My adventures themselves became the achievements that I based my worth on. Old friends envied my freedom. Others claimed to admire what they saw as my courage. I had lots of stories that never failed to impress. But I was still lonely. No one knew me or who I was. Nor did I. I was too focused on my achievements, on what I did, to really know who I was without all that. I thought I was what I did! I was wrong.

12

Trying to find my way home

*In these long moments of flat, grey emptiness,
surrounded by half-dead old people whose spirits
I cannot seem to locate, I begin to question if I
made the right choice deciding to live rather than
surrender to death three months ago. At times like
this, life seems no more than a combination of
ignorance and suffering.*

There is a famous experiment in psychology that
demonstrates what is called learned helplessness. A dog
is locked in a cage with a wired floor and is given electric
shocks at random intervals. The dog struggles to avoid
the shocks until eventually, realising there is no escape, no
means of predicting when the shocks will come, and no way
of protecting himself, he succumbs to passive helplessness.
He stops responding at all. After months of trying, and failing,

to protect my privacy, my dignity, my individuality and the few feet of personal space allotted to me in the ward, I gave up. Like the dog in the cage I stopped trying. I whimpered and begged friends to 'get me out of here!' (which, of course, they couldn't) then fell into a depression that was beyond tears. I stopped caring. I couldn't be bothered eating, washing myself or acting strong any longer for visitors. I felt defeated and ultimately alone. More than anything, I felt trapped and exhausted.

Friends were great. They visited regularly. But this was a solo journey in a physical, mental and emotional sense. I felt as though I was being swept away by a powerful current as friends stood helplessly on the shore calling out assurances and advice. But I was in the water alone and I didn't know where it was taking me.

For endless months confined to the same bed, my days had begun and ended with a shot in the soft flesh of my belly to prevent blood clots. Every day the same shadows slowly passed across the building outside my window. My elderly ward companions wet their beds, tore at their catheters, and seemed to move between confusion, terror and utter passivity. I knew the strain it was on my friends to come so far month after month to visit. I was often whisked away for some lab work or X-rays when visitors arrived. There were no bedside phones at the hospital; I had no control of when people visited and they had no way of checking in quickly without making the long journey to the hospital. When they arrived, I in turn felt responsible to perk up and be good company, to make their long journey worthwhile, though I sometimes felt that the effort to put on a happy face was more than I could bear.

During this time a close friend tearfully confessed that the responsibility she felt to visit regularly, to keep people informed of my progress and to coordinate visits by friends had become too stressful for her and she was starting to resent it. I tried not to take on the shame of being such a burden, of being helpless and dependent. But it stuck. My greatest fear associated with being dependent was the resentment I knew it could inspire in a caregiver whose own needs weren't being met. I thanked my friend for all she had done, much of which she had initiated herself, and asked her to look after herself now. I couldn't do that for her, couldn't make it up to her. All I could do was to give her permission to take the distance she needed from my situation and from me. I felt this loss as deeply as all the others.

It was in this condition that I received a visit from a new house surgeon. House surgeons rotate their ward responsibilities so often that I had never gotten to know any of the others. This one was different. She knew that I was in trouble emotionally and that it was having a negative impact on my recovery. I was listless and depressed. I was torn between helpless compassion for the suffering of my mostly demented ward mates and with revulsion. Eventually I didn't see any difference between myself and them. Like the dog locked in a cage in those psychological experiments, I had given up and given in, passively resigned to my situation.

The house surgeon was, I'm sure, as busy as the others had been. But she came often to visit and to listen. She brought with her at each visit some glimmer of hope, some reminder that I was an intelligent, capable adult. That I was not helpless! She made up a chart of my medications, explained all of them to me and asked that I administer them to myself. It was the first time in my endless months of hospitalisation that I had been invited to be involved in my treatment. She suggested that I write down any questions or concerns as they came up so that we could cover them item by item at scheduled visits. I had many and, good to her word, she took the time to collaborate with me on a plan to get me out of the hospital with all of the home-based services that would require. She even arranged for me to be brought cake and supplemental high-calorie drinks each day to boost my weight, which had dropped to under 45 kg from the initial six weeks in hospital without food. She insisted that she was only doing her job when I poured out my gratitude. Perhaps she was. But she did it in such a way that I felt, for the first time in months, like the competent, capable, proud human being I was beginning to think was lost to me forever. Of the many experiences I had in hospital, those few weeks of personal, practical and empowering care from this house surgeon turned me around emotionally. And that had a powerful impact on my physical recovery.

Within a week or two arrangements had been made for me to have a 'trial run' to see how I might cope outside of the hospital environment. I was to be taken out by my physiotherapist. It meant dressing in my own clothes and riding in a car for the first time since the accident. Until that time I had neither been outside of the hospital nor breathed fresh air other than on one or two occasions when friends managed to borrow a wheelchair and take me out to the footpath.

The day of my outing finally came. My friends brought

me some clothes and I felt immediately transformed, as though my street clothes gave me a status and dignity that marked my passage back into the world. I chewed my lower lip and furrowed my brow in concentration as I tied the bows in my shoelaces. It was hard work with my left hand in a cast, but I refused help. Dressing myself and tying my own shoes was yet another milestone in my recovery. Then the physiotherapist wheeled me out of the hospital for my trial run. I needed to be reintroduced to the world she said. Needed to learn how to manoeuvre in and out of a car and to feel safe on the road again.

Getting in and out of the car was a surprisingly difficult task. I had to hold on to the door as I lowered my weight onto the seat. This was complicated by the fact that I had a cast on my wrist, limited extension of my right arm and no strength in my thighs to hold my weight as I lowered myself down. But I was eager to get going. I wasn't frightened to be on the road with other cars. I was too excited about being out in the world again.

I was passing this trial run with flying colours, so the physiotherapist took me to a shopping mall where I could be around normal, healthy people doing normal everyday things. She talked me through another complicated manoeuvre — getting out of the car and into a wheelchair. I wanted to buy a small notebook, I remember, to keep track of my appointments and medications. The physiotherapist wheeled me into a stationery shop where I discovered just how little the world caters for the handicapped. I couldn't reach items on the shelves that are normally at eye level, couldn't get past displays placed in the aisles and I couldn't turn around.

Had I been on my own, I would have been trapped at the end of the aisle in my wheelchair! That was enough for me. I paid for my notebook and got out of that confined space into the open area where people casually milled about looking into shop windows.

I was enjoying the contrast to the white walls, white uniforms, white sheets and white nightgowns of the hospital, glad to be out of there, when I heard a woman walking past me whisper loudly to her friend, 'Look at her! The poor thing!' I swung around automatically to see who she was talking about. It hadn't occurred to me that it could be me. The shock of it stunned me. In a flash, I realised that my passage back into the world held challenges I hadn't considered. In the hospital all of us were in some way disabled and my disfigurement didn't seem to stand out. All of a sudden I saw myself as others saw me, disabled and disfigured, an object of pity. I wanted to go 'home', to the hospital, where I was normal. I couldn't face the world and it, apparently, couldn't face me.

The house surgeon didn't let me fall back into despair. She encouraged me to wear street clothes during the day rather than my nightgown and even suggested that I get a friend to bring me a bottle of wine for the occasional drink before dinner! 'It will increase your appetite,' she assured me. With the occupational therapist, she organised the adjustments that would be needed to make my house handicap-friendly without making it look like a hospital. A special La-Z-Boy chair was bought, a hand-held shower, a bath chair, a raised toilet seat, handrails to help me get up the stairs, a bedside commode, a food tray on wheels and even a pocket-sized phone so I could call for help if I fell. A physiotherapist, home nurse and home help were organised. The house surgeon even intervened to help me apply for a government benefit to help cover my cost of living. My GP was informed about my accident and overseeing of my care after discharge was handed over to her. I was given taxi vouchers for medical visits and a schedule of follow-up medical appointments. I was involved in every aspect of this planning, from the colour of my new chair to practise with using the home aids that I needed. There was an air of excitement where only weeks earlier I felt hopeless and helpless. Meanwhile, friends did all they could to move my belongings back into my house in the city from the beach house where I lived before the accident. Within weeks of my serious emotional decline I was on my way home to my own house, surrounded by my own things, and only minutes away from friends.

13

Home at last

Now we were improved and needed the world and life, but could not face, would be destroyed by, the fundamentals of life and the bustling, callous, careless hungriness of the world.
— Dr Oliver Sacks, *A Leg To Stand On*

All around me on the trip from the hospital to my house I saw people doing the most normal things — driving, walking, shopping, gardening — and I knew that I could do none of those things. I felt separate from a world that was once so familiar, where people mindlessly went about their business unaware of the precious miracle of their easy physicality.

Arriving home was not as I expected it to be, a time of celebration and freedom. There were only three steps to the front door, but they were more challenging than a cliff face might have been only a few months earlier. I wobbled, I groaned, I whimpered and I cried. I stood paralysed before them, leaning on my crutches.

'I can't do it!' I whispered to the physiotherapist. 'I can't! They're too high!' I realised in that moment the true extent of how much I had lost and how far I still had to go. Getting out of the hospital was not the end of the journey, nor even nearly so.

At first I felt no more in control of my time or personal space at home than I did at the hospital. People had the habit of dropping in at their convenience rather than mine, though I was now accessible by phone. One day someone from the diagnostic lab showed up in the middle of my physiotherapy treatment. She was a day earlier than appointed, but assumed that since I was housebound it didn't matter when she came. I had to stop my physiotherapy long enough to have her take blood samples. Soon after that the district nurse showed up and, because she was in a hurry, she put an end to my physiotherapy treatment altogether. I felt abused and helpless all over again. Even some friends seemed to expect that I somehow play the gracious hostess now that I was home, although I could not even manage to prepare a cup of tea for myself.

I felt overwhelmed by the sheer magnitude of energy that visitors brought into the house with them. Without the long ride to the hospital, friends popped in frequently without the reserve of people entering a hospital ward. They couldn't slow down and I simply could not get up to their speed. Though I felt the love that came through my door with each visit, I felt the difference — and the distance — that now existed between us. I was overwhelmed by the complexity of trying to interact with more than one person at a time and terrified of the implicit demand, now that I was home, that I appear somehow 'normal' in my interactions, though I couldn't quite remember how to do that. I found myself resenting the mindless innocence with which people seemed to make their way through life. My contempt was merely a reflection of my envy, knowing that that innocence was lost to me forever.

There were times when I was so overwhelmed I just wanted the world to go away and leave me alone. I got up early one day to receive a visit from out-of-town friends who were in Auckland. Between 8 a.m. and 10 a.m. two other friends who didn't know each other dropped by, my home help came to visit, another friend came, my mother phoned from the States, and the repairman arrived to fix my television. They all wanted my attention! A neighbour came to offer her phone number just as a friend called for some information. I asked my friend to call back. I was barely coping with all that was going on. But she insisted that she needed the information right away. I felt on the verge of panic! My out-of-town friend meanwhile quietly cleaned up for me, changed the bed and nudged another into moving a plant for me. She alone understood. She got it! I cried when they all left. I cried and pulled the plug out of the phone and climbed into bed.

Beyond the walls of my house it was painful to watch strangers respond to my disability rather than to me. To see the pity, the embarrassment, the generosity that would otherwise not have been directed towards me. On my first day out of the house for anything other than a medical appointment I went to my neighbour to see if I could borrow something. He had a friend visiting and explained me to his friend rather than introduced me. I had the feeling that he was a bit embarrassed to be associated with me and that he needed to somehow distance himself. That same day, a friend drove me to a building supply store where I was offered an unsolicited discount on my purchase. It felt as though it was all — the pity and the generosity — a response not to me but to whatever discomfort my disability and disfigurement triggered in them. I felt more shame than gratitude and couldn't wait to return to the safe, anonymity of my own home. And that's where I stayed.

By mid-December I had been out of the hospital and homebound for four months. Long enough! I decided to go Christmas shopping with the assistance of a home help to drive and carry my bags. I was still on two crutches. With the best of intentions and what Christmas cheer I could muster, I set out determined to find gifts for friends who had been there for me when I needed them. I wanted to come back out of hiding and join the world in the spirit of Christmas. But, confronted with fast-moving crowds, Christmas carols blaring from loudspeakers and traffic lights that changed faster than I could cross the street, my resolve shattered. An ambulance sped by with its sirens screaming. I froze. Then I broke down and began to tremble and cry in the middle of the street. 'I want to go home,' I whimpered. 'I can't do this.' I felt assaulted. The home help hadn't noticed anything unusual and seemed confused by my reaction. I knew I couldn't explain. There was nothing unusual about the scene that assaulted my senses. It was my perspective of the world as a chaotic and dangerous place that was unusual. Until that time I had wondered how I could possibly remain in touch with the infinite or divine and be fully engaged in the world at the same time. Now I began to fear that I may never again be able to remain in touch even with my own centre when confronted with the chaos of the world beyond my front door.

For years afterwards, I wore my physical vulnerability like a radar, on guard constantly against any possibility of injury. I felt myself to be no more physically secure than a shattered porcelain cup carefully glued together. The sight of a five-year-old running to hug me or a dog loping on the beach in my direction was enough to make me freeze in terror. Once, after several months of being back home, the unthinkable happened. I fell! I tripped on the carpet and screamed as I thrust my still-healing wrist out to break my fall. My forehead hit the wall and I landed huddled on the floor sobbing uncontrollably. I wasn't hurt . . . at all! But the terrible certainty that I was about to hurt myself and that this time, like Humpty Dumpty, nothing and no one would ever be able to put me back together again, was so overwhelming that my body responded as if the threat was real. I was shocked not to be hurt. The effect was the same heart-stopping, breathless disbelief one might experience having missed a serious accident by a matter of inches or seconds.

I didn't break! I really was OK!

14

From doing to being

Friends ask what I'm doing these days. This is one of the ways of defining ourselves and giving our lives meaning that I no longer have available to me. I'm housebound. What I do is wait. Like a kid in a car on a long journey, I just watch the scenery outside my window speed by and wonder when I'm going to get wherever it is that I'm headed. Every time I have to admit that I don't 'do' much of anything, I feel ashamed. It is an answer that places me clearly on the outside.

The 'doing' part of my life now consisted of organising all of the things that were done to and for me. Every day home helps came to the house to cook, clean, shop, do laundry . . . All the chores I would so love to have been able to do for myself. Each week the osteopath, physiotherapist and psychologist came to treat me at home and every now and then the district nurse or my doctor came by to check on me. I was taken to the hospital several times a month for clinic visits and had to arrange transportation for that. And, of course, friends dropped by and called. The rest of the time I slept or read or wrote or watched television.

When I was not doing or being done to, I was simply being. This is a highly underrated skill that most either don't possess or possess in very short supply. Following the sun from one end of the couch to the other, soaking up the warmth and drinking in the richness of the colours filtering through the crystal that hung in the window. Noticing the texture of the flowers at my back door. My senses felt alive. How often I noticed the sound of my own breath or of a bird in the back garden singing. Things I was too busy to notice before.

For a long time I felt much slower than the rest of the world. I felt calm and centred and somehow rarely distracted from the moment. When friends came by to visit it was hard to 'come out' of myself to meet them, though I truly wanted to be with them. It was as though I lived in a very different world from them. It was slower, richer, calmer, more full of detail, less full of activity. There was a separateness about it too — sort of being 'in' the world but not 'of' it. It was a separateness that I knew I couldn't maintain. I had chosen to live, to come back to the reality of activity, but it was like knowing it's time to get up before you're quite ready. It takes time. The fear was always there that once 'awake' I would either forget the dream — the rich quality of everyday things — or it would lose its impact. Meanwhile, the phone was ringing, I was making lists, and the cab was about to pick me up for my next hospital appointment. The better I got, and the busier, the narrower my focus and my experience of life became.

I could see why 'enlightened' beings tended to hang out in caves or monasteries. The world seemed so demanding, so distracting, so caught up in comforting illusions — illusions mostly born of fear. Am I good enough? Smart enough? Rich enough? Attractive enough? Capable enough? Busy enough? The list goes on. It all has to do with the fantasy of control and the belief that we are much smaller — much more narrowly defined — than we really are.

I found myself trying to understand how (or even if) it was possible to be fully human and keep the infinite — the divine — in perspective. Just the fact that I was trying to figure it out instead of simply allowing myself to know the answer was a real shift in consciousness from where I had been only a few short months earlier. The infinite cannot be understood! It certainly can't be contained. It's laughable that I even tried.

I felt like a child that had grown old overnight because of an experience that none of the other 'kids' around me had ever had. I recognised in them an innocence that was once mine and knew that the world looked different to them than it now did to me. There was an immediacy about their world, an urgent and unbridled energy that I found demanding, exhausting and almost always distracting no matter how much I loved them or how much joy they gave me. I found it difficult to keep my senses alive and opened around other people. Eventually I found myself shutting down my sensibilities and narrowing my focus in order to cope.

Some months after I got out of the hospital, a friend took me back to the beach where I had lived before the accident. It was my first non-medical outing in more than six months since the accident and I was overjoyed at the prospect. It was only a few feet from the car to the beach, where my friend had to lower me like a sack of potatoes onto the sand in front of that wild, magnificent ocean. I was drinking it in. The warm soft sand in my fingers, the pounding surf, the wind and haze and sun . . . All the while, she was talking about work! It was as though she was somewhere else, missing the whole thing and pulling me away from it with her! I could appreciate that she wanted to give me a day out of the house and I was truly grateful for that. But as I joined her in a reality far from this beautiful place, I realised that, although we sat side by side, we inhabited entirely different worlds.

As I waited (and waited!) for recovery, I was reminded of the ten months that I had been confined to bed at the age of twelve. I was an active, bike-riding, tree-climbing, jitterbugging fan of *American Bandstand* when I came down with a severe fever and a heart murmur that the doctors could not explain. Though I had no pain, I was confined to bed twenty-four hours a day indefinitely as they tried to determine the source of the murmur. There was to be 'no excitement'. I couldn't join the family for meals or even get up to change the channel on the television. At the time I thought it anything but a positive experience. I prayed and bargained with God to let me get better, to let me play with my friends and go to school with the other kids. But to no avail. At first I got lots of attention, but my twelve-year-old friends quickly disappeared and family got on with their own lives. I waited . . .

While I waited, the person that I was to become took shape. I studied (what else was there to do?) and excelled in all of the schoolwork that tutors brought to me. I thought about life and God as few twelve-year-olds do. I wrote short stories and hand-built a huge birdcage out of toothpicks that I soaked in warm water and held in position to shape each until they dried. I watched my siblings play on the front lawn and knew, as they never could, the preciousness of their easy physicality. And I learned early on to enjoy my own company and develop my own opinions free of peer pressure. After ten months confined to bed, my irregular heart sounds hadn't changed and the doctors decided to let me return to school. But, in that time, who I was had changed. My perception of and relationship with the world would never be the same.

Years later, as I was bounding up the stairs to my bedroom two at a time, I had a flashback of being carried from the master bedroom downstairs where I spent my days, to my bedroom upstairs. In that moment I was stunned to recognise how far I'd come since those days and how much that experience had shaped who I'd since become. I celebrated my physicality, my independent thinking, adventurous spirit and academic achievements. I have often considered it to have been one of the most positive times of my life, though I certainly would never have said so at the time!

Admittedly, I wore a social mask to fit back in with the other kids when eventually I returned to school. Most of the kids weren't as introspective or intellectually curious as I had become. Certainly not as philosophical! I ratted my hair and smoked cigarettes and tried to look cool. I had recovered from the experience, but it stayed with me and, underneath the cover, the image I wore, it shaped me. Thirty-five years later, I needed to believe that the same creative process was repeating itself and that one day I would realise the rewards and not just the awful cost of this experience.

My life was full of wonderful outdoor activities and adventures.

Two months before the accident. I was 47 and life was looking good.

The fireman who cut me out of the car said that only my head and shoulders were visible in the twisted wreckage.

The impact of my face striking the steering wheel was so great that it shattered the bones of my face and bent the steering wheel.

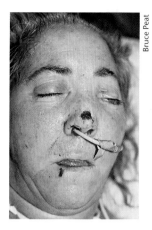

ABOVE LEFT: The bones of my face were shattered with only swelling to give it shape. Miraculously, my face had only two small cuts.

ABOVE RIGHT: A machine breathed for me through a hole cut in my throat.

RIGHT: Part of my calf muscle and a skin graft covered the hole in my leg. A heavy 'fixater' screwed into my shin held the bones in place for several months.

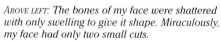

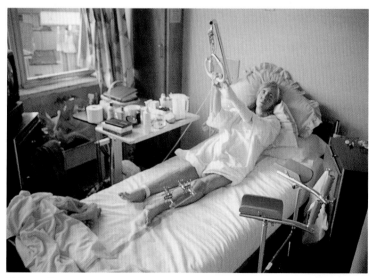

This small space was my entire world for four months.

When I finally returned home, climbing my front steps seemed an impossible task.

It had been four months since the accident, but I looked twenty years older.

I taught myself to use a computer with my wrist in a cast.

A few days before my first private surgery. I hoped my reflection in the mirror would become more familiar.

One month after surgery.

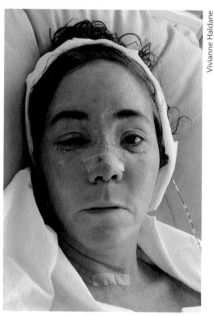

The morning after surgery. Swelling keeps the real outcome hidden.

Vivianne Haldane

Brace-less at last on Muriwai beach.

Mom and I have become great friends.

I rented a house for a weekend in Muriwai to celebrate my fiftieth birthday and to thank friends whose love I could not have done without. (Not everyone is present in the photo.) In the eight years since that photo was taken, two of the married couples broke up, one friend's partner died suddenly, one friend disappeared and is presumed dead, two couples unexpectedly became first-time parents late in life, and the children of two single parents grew up and left home. Each lost something basic to their identity. Such transitions are life-changing and not at all uncommon.

The entrance I created to what I thought would be my little piece of paradise in Guatemala.

The beautiful view from the verandah of my little casita. Something much more complex lies beneath this tranquil image.

Eleven years on. Life is looking good again!

15

Helpers

Everyone tells me that I must lower my expectations of what I can do. 'Supporting' me by denying my giant — my power, my vitality. Instead I feel disabled! The expectation that I am less able than I was, less capable, makes it all the harder to regain my sense of competence. I want to focus on what I can do and what I want to do instead of on what I can't do. I want to celebrate and build on what I have accomplished rather than simply accept that it is 'good enough'. Yet I am so tired. So easily disheartened. I have not only to recover, but it seems that I have to fight the world to do it.

Ever since I can remember, it was I who held the more or less safe status of helper in relation to others. I was always the one who friends came to with their fears and insecurities, their disappointments and despair. In high school I was the one who both boys and girls came to talk to about their romantic relationships. It wasn't that I was an expert on having a successful relationship. I was simply a good listener who had a knack of asking the right questions to help others find their own answers. Later, as a young high school teacher, students came to detention after school just to hang out and talk with me. Some were not even in my classes! They just came to open up and be listened to. I liked that. Eventually I became a professional helper.

What I was not skilled at was recognising my own needs and vulnerabilities. I was too busy helping others, safe in the false belief that I didn't need help. When I did need help (as, of course, I did) I didn't know how to ask for it. I demanded it. Felt it was a right rather than a need. I resented ever having to rely on others and held such high expectations that I was usually disappointed in the help I did receive. It was a vicious circle, but one I didn't recognise. So long as my helpers were inadequate to meet my expectations, my determination to not rely on anyone but myself remained strong. I prided myself on this independence, though I know now that it was based not on my strengths but on my fear of depending on others. Not surprisingly, although I had many friends and was successful at my work, I never sustained a long-term committed relationship with any one partner. I told myself that no single person could be enough for me. But the truth was that the two most important men in my life — my father and the love of my life — had taught me that emotional dependence was too great a risk to my self-esteem.

So, when I found myself helplessly dependent on

strangers for my most basic needs and on my friends and family for continued love and support, I was terrified. And I was furious! To find myself so demoted in status. How do I do this? I had no idea. From the beginning, I saw inadequacy all around me, though in reality it was often just the fact that the hospital was filled with hundreds of others with needs as important and often more urgent than my own. I saw the helpless old women who shared my ward mumble, 'Thank you dear,' when nurses arrived perhaps a half-hour later to remove their bedpan. When I was left on a bedpan for that long I wanted to scream my rage at the pain and indignity of it all. Didn't they know? It was hard enough to have to ask for help, but to call for help and not be responded to when my bladder was full or my food tray left out of reach, felt cruel. I didn't know how not to take it personally. How did this happen to me?

I tried to reclaim the familiar helper/teacher role. I explained patiently to nurses who left me waiting on a bedpan that, with two broken legs, it hurt. Perhaps if they just waited the thirty seconds it took for me to relieve my bladder? I asked aides to please leave the food tray within my reach and a nurse to remove a bandage on a new surgical wound that was soaked with soapy water from the sponge bath she had just given me. No one wanted a patient telling them how to do their job. Years later I presented a formal proposal to the hospital, as a psychologist and former patient, to train medical staff on the important role of the relationship between medical staff and patients in the healing process. I was told that it would be 'unethical to have a patient train staff'. The demoted status of patient was apparently officially sanctioned and overrode my professional status as a psychologist.

What a difference it would make if every doctor and nurse had the experience of being a patient and every therapist had the experience of being a client! As a therapist myself I knew only too well the human limits of the 'experts' in that role. My first therapist was a hospital psychologist who visited me whenever he could at my bedside in the ward. Our 'privacy' consisted of a cotton curtain pulled around my bed. Though I knew that the other patients and their guests and even the hospital aides could hear me, I cried to him of my fear, my indignity and exhaustion at trying to protect myself from what sometimes felt to me like the indifference of my caregivers. He'd been sent to help me in my distressed state. I was losing weight and not getting better. And, I'm sure on some level, he was sent to fix the problem patient that I had become for some of the staff.

One day the therapist arrived and wheeled me into an empty room, bed and all, 'For a more private session,' he said. I knew something was up! There he gave me a pep talk about team spirit and urged me to support my team-mates, the staff. I knew he was like the meat in the sandwich. I was looking to him to get staff to understand the emotional needs of patients. To see and respond to us as individuals in an alien and frightening environment. They were looking to him to convince me to accept the passive role of the patient a bit more graciously.

'One thing I've learned from this experience,' I told him, 'is that all my energy needs to go into getting better and being authentic is an essential part of that. I don't have the energy to pretend for the sake of others any more. I can't take care of anyone else right now! I'm the patient. They're supposed to take care of me.'

The social graces we normally expect from one another, often in the form of a pleasant mask hiding our feelings, was a burden I couldn't afford. If I hurt, I wanted to cry. If I had a physical complaint (like a broken wrist) I wanted to let people know and have it taken seriously. If I couldn't command respect in my hospital gown, I wanted at least some compassion for my dis-ease and tolerance for the distress it might cause those in charge of my care. Like a drowning person, I thrashed about trying to keep my head above water. I wasn't always easy to be around. Drowning people never are.

Years later I would use this experience to develop a workshop titled 'The Helpless Helper' for volunteers and professionals working with people in crisis. How often, when comforting others do we use expressions such as 'Don't cry' and 'It's all right'? When we love someone we want their pain and fear to go away. The same is true of people whose job it is to help. Helpers often need those they're trying to help to be all right in order to feel successful in their roles as helpers.

Denial, bargaining, anger. These are generally accepted stages of grief. Yet, often it's the helper, feeling helpless in the face of his or her desire to make everything all right, who unconsciously displays these stages of grief in the helping relationship. Without being aware of it, the needs of the helper to feel helpful can pressure the 'helpee' into the position of caring for the caregiver — of hiding or withholding emotions that, unattended, can interfere with physical as well as emotional recovery.

'Everything's all right,' they may say. 'Shush, don't cry.' They might deny the loss further with assurances such as, 'You can get another one.' Another best friend or spouse. Another job. A replacement limb. Even a replacement child. All of which may be true and none of which gives room to grieve the loss of what was.

Bargaining can just as easily block the emotional expression of the person being helped. Parents have been trained to distract children from pain or loss with treats. Doctors give lollies to children to stop their tears. We all do it, or have done at some time. Wishful thinking is another kind of bargaining and can easily come across as blame. 'If only you hadn't . . .', 'I wish he had . . .', 'If only I'd been there.'

When the painful feelings continue to be expressed, the helpers — the mothers, the teachers, the doctors or nurses or therapists or friends — can eventually get frustrated in their attempts to help. Even the most loving of us are likely to experience anger. 'Stop that crying!' 'Just get over it!' 'I can't work miracles, you know!'

Helping is a relationship between human beings. Both bring human needs and strengths to the relationship. The helper needs to feel helpful. But if that need is put before the needs of the person seeking help, the relationship is in danger of becoming competitive and someone will lose.

Several weeks after I was moved from intensive care to an orthopaedic ward, a young registrar was called in to find a vein that would accept yet another IV line. My veins had collapsed and my drip was no longer passing important fluid into my body. He was obviously rushed and increasingly frustrated in his attempts to get a line working. As he repeatedly struggled to force an IV tube where it wouldn't go, I cried out in pain and he snapped, 'I didn't become a doctor so I could hurt people!' He threw down the IV tube and stormed out of the room, leaving me whimpering. He was young and he was supposed to be the expert, I knew. My uncooperative veins and exhausted cry had undermined his confidence and, as so often happens, he took it out on me. The following day when I saw him, I called him to my bedside. He approached brusquely, snapped the curtain around my bed shut and seemed to be preparing himself for a rebuttal from a 'difficult patient'. I gently reminded him that, as a doctor he would see a lot of pain and would by necessity sometimes have to inflict some, but that as a patient I couldn't protect him from that. We had to cope with the pain together. His body visibly relaxed and he whispered, 'Thank you.' Then he walked rather than marched, as he had done the day before, from my bedside.

I went through five therapists in three years following the accident. I just couldn't let go of the control over my own care! 'Here's how to take care of me,' I'd try to say, collapsing in a flood of tears. 'This is what I need of you, not that.' I still don't know how good or bad that was for me (and the people there trying to help me). Having lost control over everything else, I needed more than anything to feel competent at something, not to simply be done to like an object to be fixed in some well-studied way. I needed to assert myself as I struggled to find my self in the physical and emotional body I now inhabited. I needed gentle, personal care. But I also needed to learn how to allow myself to be cared for.

I anticipated the transference issues my therapists were looking for and knew all the 'techniques' — the tricks of the trade — that were being used. I bristled at being fitted into any particular model of therapy and found myself getting distracted by wondering how I might have responded (better?) if I were in the therapist role. I also watched my own reactions when a therapist responded in a way that I might have. Some of the clever things I did as a therapist (and that therapists did with me as their client) didn't feel all that great on the receiving end. 'So that's what it feels like when my ego gets in the way!' I'd think with a sinking feeling. All the while I was as much an observer of my care, a guardian keeping a close watch, as I was a participant.

Needing help went on long after I got out of the hospital. The counselling continued in my home as did the physiotherapy, osteopathy, lab check-ups and home visits from the doctor and visiting nurse. Home helps came in to prepare my meals, shop and clean for me and sometimes to help me bath and dress. Alone at night I knew that if I should fall or drop a crutch I couldn't pick it up or get off the floor without help. Once, tempted by the sun streaming through my living room window, I risked sitting on the couch that I knew was too low for me. I didn't have the strength in my legs to get back up. Trapped on the couch! It was one of those rare and wonderful moments when I laughed out loud at the absurdity of my situation. My comfy couch a dangerous trap! Happily my brain was working better than my legs. I shoved the couch cushions under my bottom one by one to give me the height to push myself off the couch with my crutches.

Something that surprised me then (but no longer does) was the discovery that so many of my paid helpers were having trouble coping with their own lives. Three of my five therapists were dealing with divorce, past or present. One even kept referring to her divorce in our sessions as she related it to my losses. 'I understand. When I got divorced I felt . . .' She was clearly unresolved and using the sessions in some way to get a grip on her own loss. I changed therapists. Finally I found a therapist who really fitted the bill for me. Only one week after I made the commitment to myself and to her to allow myself to receive the help I knew I needed, to surrender my need to control the process, her mother died unexpectedly, forcing her to leave the country for an extended period! I was caught by the irony of it. To have made the decision that I would give up control — in this particular situation and with this particular person — only to have that decision overruled by circumstances outside of my control, I was again reminded that I wasn't in control in the first place!

Home helps who cooked and cleaned and shopped for me sometimes left because of family problems. One, a single mother between places to live and with a broken car to boot finally just didn't show up one day. Without her I could neither bathe nor prepare food for myself. I wondered if perhaps, by tending to one more helpless than themselves, some of these helpers were hiding from their feelings of helplessness to control their own lives. I didn't try to rescue any of them. Not one! In that respect, at least, I was 'cured'.

16

Jake

They drink — They drive — We die
Anti-drunk-driving slogan, Land Transport Safety Authority

All it took to tear my comfortable life to shreds was the selfish act of a stranger. 'Jake' was not the first drunk driver to wreak havoc on someone's life and I was not the first victim. The scenario is common enough. Jake was twenty-three years old and, I was told, with a blood alcohol level more than twice the legal limit, was illegally driving at night on a restricted licence. The accident was his fifth serious driving offence. Yet his permit to drive had never been revoked. Not even after a hit-and-run incident. It wasn't until five months after the accident that Jake appeared in court for the first time to offer his plea. By then I had undergone at least five operations and spent four months in hospital while he legally continued to drive. He was charged with driving with excess blood alcohol, causing bodily injury while under the influence of alcohol and careless driving causing injury. The local constable knew him well and called to tell me the outcome of the court hearing. Jake had entered a plea of 'no plea', which gave him at least another month behind the wheel of a car before he would be asked again for his plea.

I cried at the news. 'Innocent until proven guilty,' the constable apologised. He had been at the scene of the accident and knew what had happened to me. Knew Jake's history and his blood alcohol level at the time. He admitted his frustration that prior offences were treated so lightly. So far as I knew, the worst consequence of Jake's driving record had been to extend his remaining time on a restricted licence. Typically the courts at that time didn't treat driving offences severely. It was easy in those days for anyone whose licence had been revoked to drive on a friend's licence because a licence to drive offered no photo and no more detail of the driver than date of birth. I was afraid Jake would someday kill himself or someone else unless he was stopped. I wasn't far wrong.

Four months earlier, shortly after I got out of intensive care, I had asked to meet Jake. No one could understand why I would want to meet the person who had done this to me. But I knew that this was one of the most significant events of my life and that I could not allow it to remain anonymous. I sent word to Jake through people I knew from the area we both lived in that I didn't hate him and that I wanted to meet. What happened that night was personal. This was no abstraction. He had changed my life and I wanted him to see the person, the flesh and blood consequences of his behaviour. I wanted somehow to change his life. I believed that if he met me in person and that if I approached him as a person rather than the monster that my mother was so sure he was, I might be able to stop him from ever doing this kind of harm again. If I could do that, I reasoned, then this would be less of a tragedy. Something good would have come of it. Somehow, by helping Jake to change so that he would never do this to anyone else, I felt that I was helping myself.

Not long after I put word out that I wanted Jake to meet me, a police officer came to the hospital to see me. He was responding, he explained, to a report from Jake saying that he'd heard that I didn't blame him for the accident. I think I laughed. 'Oh no!' I told the policeman, 'I said I didn't hate him. But I absolutely consider him responsible for the accident. There is a difference.' The officer understood — we both did — that Jake wanted to be let off the hook. I was advised to have a witness in the room when I met with Jake so that nothing I said would be misinterpreted. There was a danger, it seemed, that by not condemning Jake, as well as his actions, he might consider himself excused from responsibility.

The day for our meeting finally came. I hadn't slept the night before. It was so important to me that I find the right words to get through to Jake. To get him to understand rather than defend what he had done and, I feared, would continue to do until someone died. The nurses arranged to have the visitors' room empty for us to have this meeting. One volunteered to be a silent witness as the policeman had recommended. Together we waited more than an hour for him to arrive. When he didn't, I felt humiliated. I didn't hate him for the accident. To my mind that was a mindless, ignorant, selfish act. But it wasn't directed at me. I did, however, begin to hate him for standing me up in this way, for failing to face me even when I promised no angry recriminations. I cried and the nurse who was to be my witness offered to take me outside in a wheelchair for some fresh air (a rare treat) while she ate lunch.

As she wheeled me down the hospital corridor, a lanky youth on crutches and an older woman stopped us to ask where Kathy Torpie's room was. Instantly I knew that this was Jake. This awkward, lanky country boy who looked no more than a teenager was the one who had inflicted all this damage on me! A moment earlier I was seething with anger at him for his failure to show up. I knew that if he saw that anger he would shut down and nothing I had to say would touch him. I wanted to yell at him for putting me through this, for being more than an hour late for such an important occasion.

'I thought you weren't coming,' I managed. The woman with him immediately offered an excuse.

'There was a lot of traffic.'

We changed direction and headed to the visitor's room. At the door I explained to the woman who I assumed to be Jake's mother or grandmother that I wanted to speak with Jake alone. That this was something that happened to the two of us and what I had to say was personal. She jumped in protectively again.

'You have a support person. I don't see why Jake shouldn't.'

I explained that the nurse was a silent witness, not a

support person. Then I turned to Jake. 'Do you need your mother for support, Jake?' There was something mocking in my voice, I knew. This was my challenge. He looked at the floor and shook his head, No. It was ludicrous for anyone to think that this young man needed protection from me. I was in a wheelchair with bolts sticking out of my leg, ugly red scars on my arm and legs, a wired jaw, flattened face, hair that was stringy from so much anaesthetic, and a patch over my left eye.

There was a moment of silence when the door closed behind us. Jake stared at the floor and mumbled, 'I have to tell you that I don't remember anything about that day.' I imagined that this was his lawyer speaking.

'Well, you were pretty drunk,' I offered.

'No, it's because of a head injury,' he insisted. 'I don't remember anything about that day. I don't even remember drinking.'

'OK,' I said, 'let me fill you in.' And I went on in a calm voice to tell him about who I was and what I had been doing that evening. About my move to Muriwai and my new life as a writer. I told him about the injuries in detail and about the shock and pain my family and friends had to go through. But his eyes never left the floor. I asked where he was headed at that time of night. I hadn't expected to see traffic coming out of Muriwai (where there is only one road in and out). Without a pause he told me exactly where he was headed. He remembered all right!

I leaned forward in my wheelchair and reached my hand toward him. 'Give me your hand, Jake.' He looked up then, frightened, it seemed to me, and confused.

'Why don't you hate me?' he almost cried. I explained that I had a lot of other things to cope with and didn't need hate on top of it all.

'Jake, you're not a bad person. But you are dangerous. What you did was stupid and self-centred. But you never intended to hurt anyone.' Then I removed the patch over my left eye that sat low and at an angle on my cheek and handed him a photo taken of me laughing only a few months earlier.

'This is what I looked like before the accident and this is the face I have to live with now. You didn't mean to do this, but you did it and now we both have to live with it.' The contrast between the person in the photo and the one holding his hand was striking. As he stared at the photo, tears welled up in his eyes.

'You never have to do this again, Jake. You have a choice!' I insisted.

He looked up at me and asked, 'How come something so terrible had to happen for me to see that I've got to change?'

'If you do change, then this whole thing will be that much less of a tragedy,' I replied. By now we were both teary. He thanked me and I made sure to tell him that this didn't mean that I didn't want him to be punished for what he did but that I hoped he would use his punishment in some positive way. We were still holding hands when we left the room, each to begin the rest of our lives. 'I got through to him!' I thought with relief, then returned to my room to fall into a deep and welcome sleep.

So four months later, when Jake entered 'no plea', I was

devastated. I felt utterly dismissed, my experience swept conveniently under some carpet of fear or cowardice. I wanted to blame the justice system that waited so long after the fact to bring it to court. I was certain that if he had pleaded right after our meeting he would have admitted his guilt and would have made a giant leap forward in his life by doing so. Instead he was allowed to continue to drive and, I heard through the grapevine, continue to drink. A month following the first hearing he entered 'no plea' once again, saying he had a new lawyer and hadn't had enough time for a plea. And with that he was back on the road again. I was still homebound, still requiring home help to get by. Another month went by and, forced to make a definitive plea, Jake pleaded 'not guilty'. It was on the day of my forty-eighth birthday. 'How could he?' I sobbed. 'He saw me! He saw what he did. How could he look me in the face and then plead not guilty to save his own neck?' The constable, who was still in touch with me, explained that by doing this he was guaranteed to be able to continue to drive over the Christmas and summer holidays since the court wouldn't reconvene until February. My heart stopped. Muriwai is a holiday destination with access by only one road. The road Jake lived on. 'He'll kill someone,' I choked.

I was told that Jake had already been stopped again — since the accident — for driving illegally. But he couldn't be disqualified without a trial. There was nothing that the police or prosecutors could do. Eight months after the accident, Jake had still not yet been to trial nor been restricted in any way. On Christmas Day he drove drunk down the wrong side of the road and collided into a rock wall, totalling his car. His trial was still six weeks away. And by New Zealand law, he could legally continue to drive until then.

I knew that in other western countries evidence of drunk driving was sufficient to disqualify drivers before they come to trial. Commonly, refusal to be tested is sufficient reason in itself to disqualify a person suspected of drunk driving. In some cases cars are even confiscated from repeat offenders. But that was not the case in New Zealand. It was only luck that no one else was injured by him while he awaited trial. Had someone, rather than a wall, been in his way on Christmas Day, there would have been another family in mourning. It might even have been his own.

It took the accident on Christmas Day to get Jake to change his plea to guilty and it took putting him in jail to get him off the road. He was sent to a prison farm in the country for six months. I think he served three. Though I wrote to him on the anniversary of the accident, reminding him that my life continued to be a series of surgeries and asking him not to risk drinking and driving again, I never heard from him and never knew if anything had changed for him after all.

17

Waiting

I'm no longer content to sit quietly and enjoy the finer subtleties in life — the flowers, birds, the sun shining through the prism. I've lost my appreciation, my quiet joy, even my interest in life.

During my long stay in the hospital and much of my recovery time at home, I often found myself almost entirely absorbed by the moment, fully experiencing the richness of the sounds and sensations it provided. It was a kind of enforced meditation. Sometimes an entire day would pass in the hospital and I would realise that I had spent a good deal of it watching the shadows slowly make their way along the wall of the building outside of my window. I learned that, like many of my elderly ward companions, I too could sometimes 'leave' the ward by simply engaging my imagination or closing my eyes and giving into the sounds of

Enya, Pachelbel or Gregorian chants on my Walkman. I knew too that, unlike my ward companions, I was fortunate to be able to choose these moments of escape from the hospital.

Back in my home, eating lunch might take as long as an hour as I slowly chewed my food, savouring the taste and texture. My ability to smell, and with it, my ability to taste most things, had only recently returned. Between bites I might stop to focus on a bird struggling to pull a juicy worm from my garden and silently wonder if he was enjoying his lunch as much as I was. I enjoyed the colour, texture and fine details of the flowers closest to my opened French windows and appreciated my cosy home when listening to the sound of rain falling on my corrugated-iron roof. There were often times of great contentment. I loved feeling fresh air coming through open doors, seeing the garden just beyond, having telephone access to friends and family whenever I liked, eating what I liked when I liked, and being in my own space. All of the things that are so painfully absent when living in a hospital ward.

I could indulge myself in the richness of each moment because, with so much alone time, I was free to do so. Free, in a sense, because I couldn't do anything else! Rushing was no longer part of my life. I didn't have to schedule myself for weekend retreats, as some of my friends occasionally did for a meditative top-up before making their way back to the city, through Sunday night traffic, and rushing headlong into Monday morning and the demands of their everyday lives. I can't take credit for my long periods of meditation and contemplation or for the blessedness of knowing what it is to live in the moment. I wasn't searching for some enlightened state. I was forced to stop, forced to be taken care of, and forced to spend time engaged with my self and my environment. Something I might not otherwise have done. I had all the time in the world and, naturally, I moved at a much slower pace through my day.

But, the better I got, the less content I felt. Halfway between housebound and free, between injured and well, I was neither. No longer meditating or whiling the hours away in contemplation. I was waiting! Waiting for the next meal, for the next medical appointment, the next operation, the next stage of my recovery. Waiting, more than anything, for the time to come when I could finally stop waiting! When my mind pulled at me, my thoughts demanding attention, there were times of immense frustration. This was my time of 'being hung on a hook' as Inanna had been, while I waited for my future to unfold.

Waiting is the opposite of being in the moment. It might look the same to an observer, quiet and inactive, but it's a whole lot different. Sometimes after brushing my teeth, bathing, and having breakfast, I found myself waiting for the day to end. Time became a burden I couldn't bear as my energy returned and I remained in a kind of social vacuum, separate from the world beyond my front door. I eventually gave way to anger as I waited, feeling the months drag on and drag me down. I shifted between the utter fascination of living in the moment and the torture of yearning for a future without casts or crutches or metal rods holding me together. Sometimes I despaired that such a future would never come. And, if it did . . . what then?

When I was less able, people came to me — to visit, to

take care of me, to cook and clean, and to heal me. Once I could take care of myself, I felt that it was no longer OK to be looked after or even to be at home all of the time. But, because I couldn't walk more than a few minutes or do any of the outdoor activities that I had once shared with friends, I couldn't join in any more. I couldn't keep up. And, I discovered, I didn't want to. Because I now had a choice, because I could get out but chose not to, I felt as though I had gone from being contemplative to being a 'couch potato'. When at last I was cast-less, brace-less, and crutch-less, I bought a car. An old 1980 Ford Escort that was built like a Sherman tank! For the first time in nine months I could get out of the house and down the front steps without help. Yet with this new freedom to go out, I found myself more bored, more restless, than I had been for most of the previous nine months. Go where? Do what?

One morning I woke with the thought, 'Life is what happens while you're waiting to die.' I knew then that I had to find my way back into the world. With an entire lifetime facing me and the awful weight of now having to make my hard-won recovery somehow worthwhile and meaningful, I found that I could no longer hold the moment as I once had. Able to visit friends in their lives now, rather than simply receive them as guests as I convalesced, I was confronted again with what I had lost and with yearnings that I didn't want to feel. While visiting friends who lived in the country one weekend, I confessed to my journal:

> *Seeing Carol tan and fit, her small tight body a reminder of something I'll never have again . . .*

Seeing her squat low in the garden as she plants,
comfortable in her body and strong . . . I can hardly
watch. And I can hardly take my eyes off her. I want
that back! I want my body back!

I still wasn't at home in my body. I couldn't just roll over in bed onto one knee to reach up and turn the light off. I had to work out how to manoeuvre myself into position to do the simplest things, even to get up from a low toilet. How hard it was then to remind myself that only six months earlier I couldn't even stand up to get to a toilet, let alone sit on it. And that not long before that someone had to wipe my bum for me.

18

60 Minutes

In therapy, as one therapist after another focused on my need to grieve my losses, I struggled with questions concerning the gifts that this event held in store. How would it change my life? How could I use it? What purpose might it serve? What opportunities or insights might it present? For, without that, with only loss and grief, this would truly be a meaningless tragedy. I had no choice but to accept that it had happened. But whether or not it was a tragedy — all loss and no gain — would depend largely on how I responded to it.

Something shifted in me when I heard that Jake had pleaded 'not guilty'. I got angry! By denying responsibility for what he had done to me, I felt that my entire experience was being discounted. For the first time since the accident, I felt personally victimised by Jake.

I would not — could not — accept the role of passive victim. It would have destroyed me. Suffering the surgeries, the physiotherapy, psychotherapy and endless clinic visits to emerge merely as a survivor, expected to carry on as if none of this had happened to me, was out of the question. It had happened! Nothing I could do would change that. It happened because Jake got drunk and got behind the wheel of a car he couldn't control, and because I happened to be in the wrong place at the wrong time. I hadn't magically created the accident for some mysterious 'karmic' reason. But I did have the choice to try to create something beneficial out of the destruction, to transform it from a tragedy into something more positive. I could choose not to be defeated as well as broken. My anger is what gave me the energy to do that. Powerless anger can eat you alive. But constructive anger can save you — and maybe even help to save a few others.

I had hoped that my meeting with Jake in the hospital would have had the power to create something good out of all that I had suffered. That by meeting me in person and seeing what he had done, he would realise that his actions had consequences far beyond how much trouble he might get in. If he never again got behind the wheel of a car drunk, other potential victims of drunk driving would be that much safer, at least from him. But I knew too that I wasn't in control of the outcome of that meeting. Other factors were at work. Inadequate drink-driving laws, a backlogged court system, Jake's relationship to alcohol and the influence of his family and friends would all help to determine how Jake responded. I had tried to stop one chronic drunk driver and I had failed.

Now I was going after a wider audience with my message. I phoned *60 Minutes* and offered them my story.

The American version of *60 Minutes* was something I grew up with. Dan Rather and Mike Wallace were relatively young men then whom I admired immensely for their investigative journalism. I had even fancied at one time becoming an investigative journalist myself. So when I phoned the New Zealand branch of *60 Minutes*, I had quality investigative journalism in mind. I told them that they could use my story as the vehicle for a piece on drunk driving in New Zealand — addressing the frequency of drunk driving incidents, the number of recidivist offenders, the devastation it causes, the social and health-related costs, and the inadequacy of the laws that govern driving offences. It was difficult to expose myself publicly like this. I asked for assurances that my story would be used to address the need for more stringent laws against drunk driving rather than for its shock value. I wasn't prepared to be exploited as a victim for sensational value when what I wanted to accomplish was so much more constructive.

I wanted to impress on others that drunk drivers and the laws that fail to control drunk drivers make all of us potential victims. To show how, when I saw Jake coming at me in my lane, I could do nothing to avoid what followed. How, although Jake had five prior driving charges against him and his blood contained twice the legal limit of alcohol at the time of the accident, the police could do nothing as he continued to drive. Their hands were tied by New Zealand law that would not disqualify a driver, regardless of his or her blood alcohol level, while they await trial. Even prosecutors could do nothing to get Jake to trial sooner as legal tactics were used to postpone the trial while he continued to endanger himself and others. We were all rendered helpless. All except the drunk driver.

A significant number of New Zealand drunk drivers re-offend, often to maim or kill. District courts see several driving-while-disqualified and driving-while-intoxicated cases every day. The police, the prosecution, the Automobile Association and Victim Support Services have all expressed their frustration at the inability of the law to protect the public from known drunk drivers — as had everyone to whom I had told my story.

So, I was excited when *60 Minutes* actually agreed to do the story. Jake may have managed to discount or deny responsibility for what he did to me. But in a way, I now felt sorry for him. I knew that I had survived and that I would move on, but that some part of him hadn't moved on and wasn't likely to until he grew up and took responsibility for his actions. Even if no positive change happened for him from this accident, he couldn't stop me from touching others. This was my opportunity to be an investigative researcher for *60 Minutes* — with my own story!

When the reporter came to my home, I had a general outline of the issues I wanted covered that went beyond my personal story and a list of facts and people who might be interviewed for the story. I told her that I was scheduled for major plastic surgery in six weeks, when the surgeon would again peel off my face, exposing my facial skeleton so that he could remove the metal plates and screws then rebuild my nose, eye sockets and cheeks. She asked if it would be possible to film the surgery in progress. That made me nervous. It felt both invasive and sensationalist. I told her no and reminded her that this was not to be sensationalised. She nodded agreement while asking if the camera crew could come in right after the surgery. I agreed.

Recording the interview was both interesting and exciting. I enjoyed the attention and felt powerful to have the media support my cause. I felt like a media insider as the crew set up in my lounge and the interviewer explained what would be happening. First the camera would be on me while she asked questions. I was to look at her, not the camera, while we talked. To pretend no one else was there. Later they would film her as she asked the same questions directly to camera. Then they would take shots of each of us separately nodding as if we were listening to the other. Later the whole thing would be pieced together by the editor. So that's how they did it!

Not long after we began the interview, the tape ran out. While the cameraman changed tapes, the interviewer commented that it was rare to find 'good talent' like me. Apparently the people they interview are often nervous and not particularly articulate in front of the camera. I knew what I wanted to say and, though not rehearsed, I found opportunities to get my point across. My 'acting' days in primary school seemed to be paying off.

The interview was going well until the interviewer leaned towards me and said in a dramatic media voice, 'I understand that at some point you — couldn't — even — control — your — own — bowels! What was that like?'

I felt an enormous pressure to answer her question. After

all, the camera was on me and waiting. Instead, to everyone's surprise, including my own, I said, 'Cut! We're not going there. This is about drunk driving. Not shock value.'

She blinked and signalled to turn off the camera. Perhaps I wasn't such 'good talent' after all. The rest of the interview went well but I was on guard and not enjoying it quite as much any more.

Weeks later, I was admitted for the first time to a private hospital for surgery. I was delighted by the contrast to public hospital. My own room with a phone, a television, my own bathroom, and a view! Of course, I wouldn't have long to enjoy many of these amenities, but their presence immediately gave the room a welcome feeling rather than one of foreboding. There was a dignity in knowing that I wouldn't have to share a bathroom with strangers and that I could talk privately on the phone.

The *60 Minutes* crew came in the following morning. I was sitting up and trying to be the articulate person that they met in my lounge. But I was still dopey and words came slowly. The cameraman positioned himself behind my shoulder as the interviewer handed me a mirror asking how I felt about the face I was looking at. The camera focused in on my reflection in the mirror. It was a swollen and bruised face, the skin pulled tightly and stapled along a line cut across the top of my scalp. It wasn't pretty. But I didn't expect it to be only hours after surgery. I gave her as much of a smile as I could manage and joked that the face I was seeing was certainly younger than I was. There were no lines, no character. I pondered aloud how we all know the feeling of one day looking in the mirror at our ageing face filled with lines from years of frowning, smiling, worrying or squinting at the sun and of wondering 'When did that happen?' This time I would be able to watch as the new character that was emerging in me etched itself into my face.

Beneath my quips about missing character lines in my face, I felt somehow exploited and ashamed. It seemed to me as if the interviewer was pushing for a provocative response to her questions. As I stared blankly at the swollen, somewhat grotesque image in the mirror with a camera awaiting my response, the interviewer asked (in the dramatic tone she had used earlier), 'How do you feel about what you see in the mirror? What would you like to say to Jake right now?'

Worried that the shock value of my story was being highlighted at the expense of the general problem of drunk driving and the laws that govern it in New Zealand, I decided to go directly back to *60 Minutes* with my concerns. I threatened to stop the story from going to air because of my concern that it would be used more for titillation than for education. To his great credit the director invited me to a meeting with him and a different interviewer to get a clear picture of what I hoped to accomplish with the story. I presented him with a proposal for the outline of the story, drunk driving statistics and a list of appropriate people to interview. He agreed to everything I asked for and even agreed to allow me to see the final story before it went to air.

Janet Wilson took over the role of interviewer. She listened carefully to what I hoped to achieve and worked with me to accomplish that. The prior interviews were done as a voice-over, with Janet narrating and cutting to me telling parts of my story. She tried to interview Jake but his mother refused to let him know that she called. 'He's already been through enough,' she told Janet. I'm sure that she was trying to protect Jake, but in doing so she both enabled his behaviour and denied him the opportunity to accept responsibility publicly for his actions or to speak out against drunk driving. I felt sorry for him. The camera followed Janet and me as we walked down the same beach where I had lived at the time of the accident as the voice-over spoke of my long recovery.

When at the end of her interview in my home Janet asked if I thought that Jake's punishment was sufficient, I replied, 'It's not about retribution. I just want Jake and others like him to understand the damage they have done so that they will never do it again!'

'Do you feel that the accident was fated?' Janet asked.

'No, because the accident didn't just happen to me,' I replied. 'It affected a lot of people. And each one of them knew that it could just as easily have happened to them.' Other things were said, but the editor ended the story right there. It was a powerful ending.

The story rated more viewers, I was later told, than any other programme all year and was nominated for a media award. I had seen it before it went to air so there were no surprises. Just a real sense of gratitude that together we were able to make such a strong statement. I viewed it with close friends on the night it aired and had a copy made to send to my family in the United States. Strangers recognised me and stopped me in the supermarket or shopping centre to congratulate me. Others wrote letters. My story had reached thousands of individuals and apparently touched many in a meaningful way. Perhaps it even made some recidivist drunk drivers reconsider whether or not it was worth the risk. I felt a powerful sense of accomplishment — of having created something positive out of the destruction — for the first time since the accident. By showing that what happened to me could have happened to any one of us, I was no longer a tragic victim of a meaningless accident. I had managed to transform the accident by giving it meaning. And in doing so I felt a return of precious dignity.

I used the fact that my story aired on television and was so well received as an opportunity to arrange a personal meeting with the Minister of Transport about the need for law change. Change has been slow, but it has come with the efforts of many others besides myself. In May 1999 the Land Transport (Drivers Licensing) Rule came into effect requiring all driving licences to have photographs. This made it impossible for those who lost their licence to simply borrow a friend's licence. Since then an amendment to the law gives officers the power to suspend automatically a dangerous driver's licence for twenty-eight days while awaiting legal proceedings. The vehicles of drunk drivers can also be automatically impounded for twenty-eight days on the spot. Legal alcohol limits have been lowered, policing is generally more stringent and . . . the road toll is down! The Land Transport (Drivers Licensing) Rule of 1999 continues to be amended to this day to make the roads safer for everyone.

I know I'm not the first person who has suffered tragic loss to put my energy into using the experience in a constructive way. Tragedy has a way of opening us up to the pain of others and of experiencing a connection through our common loss. Mothers Against Drunk Driving is an organisation made up of mothers who have lost a child because of drunk driving and have banded together to educate and change legislation in order to help prevent other mothers from experiencing the same bottomless loss. Survivors of breast cancer frequently volunteer to support women newly diagnosed with the disease. There are more organisations and private efforts to protect against further losses or to support those enduring similar losses than I can name. There is a feeling of connection with others who know what your loss feels like, in a way that even our closest loved ones can never truly understand, that helps to heal the individuals suffering the loss, even as they attempt to make the world a little bit safer or a little bit more compassionate for others in their shoes.

The *60 Minutes* programme aired on the second anniversary of my accident. The same day that my sister's son in the United States was sentenced for a drunk driving incident in which a teenage girl was killed. My nephew was about Jake's age and he too was known by local police for frequently driving under the influence. He lost his licence for ten years, and was imprisoned in a maximum security prison for a year. I am happy to report he used his experience as an opportunity to turn his life around. He no longer drinks at all. He is happily married, has a young son and a small business of his own. Neither he nor Jake were 'bad' people, just selfish, irresponsible young men and a danger to others because of that. I hope that Jake eventually used his experience to turn his life around too.

19

Plastic surgery

My pre- and post-op photos came back yesterday. Seeing how I look captured on paper took my breath away. I'm a freak! A living Picasso.

When I was released from the hospital in August, I looked twenty years older than I had four months earlier. Metal plates and screws still held the bony fragments of my facial skeleton together and the screw heads protruded beneath sagging flesh that had been stretched beyond its elastic limits. My left eye was sunken and drooped in the corner, my face was wide and flat with only the tip of a nose, my cheeks were hollow and my hair was a dull grey. The surgeon who had done my initial plastic surgery asked a more senior plastic surgeon to look in on me before my release. That surgeon suggested that I see him privately after I got out of the hospital. There was still much to be done.

We met in his office in November. There he pored over the X-rays and CAT scans before giving his attention to the 'before' photos that I so desperately shoved in his direction. Together, we compiled a list of eighteen specific problems that needed to be corrected. After looking back and forth between the photos and the flattened face before him, he said the words that I had been praying to hear. 'I may not be able to restore your face exactly as it was, but I think I can get pretty close. And,' he added, 'when I do this kind of surgery I like to finish up with a facelift.'

My friend Nicola, who had come in with me for support, and I beamed at each other! This surgeon seemed great. He gave me more than an hour of his time for the initial consultation and listened as I presented him with a long list of problems I wanted corrected and questions I wanted answered. I hung on to his words, this hope he offered that I might one day look in the mirror and see a reflection almost identical to the one that I thought I had lost forever. With a facelift, I imagined that I might even end up with a younger version of my former self! I wanted so much to believe this that I handed the surgeon my trust and, with it, my power.

Other consultations followed and an application was sent to ACC (New Zealand's nationalised insurance body) based on six to eight hours of surgery. ACC agreed to pay for the surgery based on that appraisal. All of my hope hung on believing that the surgeon could indeed accomplish all this in one surgery. The date was set when my face would be restored to me. I couldn't wait! In anticipation I had a photographer friend take some 'before surgery' photos of me so that I could compare them to my new look.

To entrust a plastic surgeon with your face — with the part of you that others generally respond to first, the part that is so essential to your ability to give your inner experience expression in the world — is an act of unspeakable faith in another human being. To put your face into the hands of someone wielding a scalpel, hammer, chisel, saw and drill with only photographs and CAT scans to guide them, you need to believe that the person understands and respects the importance to you of even minute details about the face in the photo, the face that you spent a lifetime identifying with. You need to believe that your surgeon cares about you, about what you lost and what you hope to recover. This is one area of medicine that is by its very nature deeply personal. The patient hopes to reconstruct his or her identity with that face.

The day finally came. A beautiful private hospital room. Kind, attentive staff. The surgeon came in to greet me and to let me know that he had another surgery that he had to do before my own — a patient who needed urgent surgery. I understood. How could I not? I had waited this long, a few hours would make little difference. This was my first surgery in a private hospital to be paid for by ACC. The surgeon had submitted a quote to ACC which was accepted based on surgery taking six to eight hours. I was afraid that the surgeon might rush or close me up before everything on the list was achieved if the operation took longer than planned. Just before I went into surgery, I told him that if it took longer I would pay. I was desperate to not have my surgery compromised if he ran out of time.

It was late at night when I finally woke up from surgery. I

was vomiting violently on blood and gagging on the taste as the nurse shushed me for fear that my moans would wake other patients. I had never reacted so violently to surgery before. It frightened me. I thought something was terribly wrong to see so much blood. It was not a good way to wake up.

The *60 Minutes* crew came and went. The surgeon returned to examine me and reassured me that the blood was nothing to worry about. My face was swollen and bruised as expected. I was not a pretty picture, but I remained hopeful. There was nothing to do now but to wait. Within two days I was home again, recovering again, and waiting . . . again.

It takes time before the final outcome of any plastic surgery becomes apparent. With minor soft tissue operations such as eyelid lifts, healing is generally quick and the results are clear within a week. But for reconstructive surgery, where bone as well as soft tissue is involved, the results may remain unknown for several months. While swelling decreases, bruising fades, scars heal, and skin stretched tight begins to soften, your appearance can change dramatically over a period of months following surgery. Scars can adhere to underlying tissue, giving a tethered or puckered appearance, like a pull in a piece of nylon material. Nerves can be damaged, limiting sensation and even movement. Such minor nerve damage generally repairs itself over time, but the waiting and wondering can be difficult, particularly for the inexperienced. This is the time when the doctor/patient relationship can have its most profound effect on recovery.

The follow-up appointment didn't go well. I knew it was

still early days, that it would take much longer to know the real outcome of the surgery. But it was already obvious to me that my left eye was actually lower and the corner drooped more than before. A raised right eyebrow gave me a surprised, cynical appearance. My new nose was much shorter than it had been before the accident, giving it what I thought was a piggish look. The nostrils were asymmetric and the new bridge of my nose came down in a straight line rather than in a dip between my brows. With tears in my eyes I presented the surgeon with my 'before' photos and photos taken after the surgery. The difference was blatantly obvious and disappointing. I was devastated. As far as I was concerned, I looked worse.

I felt numb realising that I would have to face surgery all over again. When I made my disappointment known, he countered that he wasn't a miracle worker. By then I knew that, of course. But I was also aware that I was still dependent on him to make things better.

In the following consultation, the surgeon urged me to be patient. To wait and see. At three months, when the swelling was well reduced, he agreed that there was indeed a need to correct the remaining problem areas originally noted in our pre-surgery consultations. He explained that the reason the operation took so long was that the nose was so badly damaged and extremely difficult to fix. But the fact remained that he had accomplished only part of what I had hoped would be achieved in almost twice the estimated time and that ACC (and I) had already paid the bill. I felt at his mercy. He assured me that the final outcome was as important to him as it was to me. I wanted to believe that. At this point

I was entirely dependent on him to do what needed to be done to make things right.

In order to complete what he originally set out to do as well as to make adjustments arising from the operation that I had hoped would be my last, he offered to put me on his waiting list at the public hospital, where there would be no additional cost to me. It would mean having my face peeled off a third time and the fragile skin under my eyes cut open again. I wanted to avoid any chance of things being left undone or done in a rush because of time constraints. I also wanted to avoid the possibility of any confused expectations. I was increasingly anxious. In the demanding modern medical environment, it is easy to get lost in the crowd. And with nationalised accident insurance, 'good enough' can easily become the standard which, because it is 'free' (which, of course it is not), should be met with gratitude. That kind of thinking can demand of patients an emotional strength and assertiveness at a time when they are at their most vulnerable if they are to get their needs met.

I went to the United States to visit family and, admittedly, to get looked after once again by my mom. While there, I read all I could about reconstructive plastic surgery at a nearby medical school library. Day after day I returned to slowly make my way through journal articles. I wanted to understand what options were available to me. Never again would I have surgery without informing myself of all my options and the risks involved with each. Finally, I came across a journal article about a woman with facial injuries very similar to mine. When I saw her photo, I was stunned. This previously attractive woman looked just like me in her post-accident, pre-surgery photos! I wasn't alone. Even more stunning were her post-operative photos. Except for a squint, she was almost exactly as she had been. I rested my head on the library desk and cried. I was convinced it could be done! Now all I had to do was find someone in New Zealand with the experience to do it.

After a bit more research, I made an appointment with one of America's most prominent reconstructive plastic surgeons for a second opinion. Knowing that I could never afford to have him operate on me, I wanted his opinion about what options he felt I had at this point and exactly what was involved. I wasn't surprised that he recommended the same procedure I had read about. What did surprise (and delight) me was the genteel, respectful way in which he listened without interruption, noting down each point I made and responding to each in turn, making sure I understood and in some cases demonstrating what he meant using a mirror, my X-rays or a model facial skeleton. It was clearly important to him that he fully understood my concerns and also that I got the information I needed to base my decisions on. As a parting comment he said something to me that carried me through many of the challenges that lay ahead.

'I've only known you briefly and will probably never see you again. But you impress me as someone with spirit and determination. Don't let anyone destroy that spirit.'

I left understanding why Dr Joseph McCarthy is held in such high esteem by patients and peers alike.

20

Anger

God give me the courage to change the things I can,
the serenity to accept the things I can't, and the
wisdom to know the difference.

— Serenity Prayer

Dr McCarthy carefully explained that my zygomatic arch (cheekbone) was in the wrong position, giving my face its lopsided appearance. He compared it to the cornerstone of a building. If the cornerstone was out of place, he explained, no amount of filling in or covering up would make the building structurally aligned. He recommended that my facial skeleton be surgically refractured and realigned before bone or fat grafts were considered to fine-tune remaining deficits. Any other approach, he warned, would camouflage rather than repair the damage. If I didn't want to undergo that kind of procedure, he suggested, I should consider trying to live with the face I had rather than trying to cover it up.

Dr McCarthy's professional reputation and the reading I had done in preparation for this appointment certainly helped me to understand and respect his opinion. But it was the doctor/patient relationship that he managed to establish with me in a single consultation that won me over. It was a collaborative relationship. It was clearly important to him that I understood the reasoning behind his recommendations and the pros and cons of various options so that I could make an informed decision, one that was right for me. I remember thinking that if I had a treasured car that was damaged in an accident, I would insist on having it repaired properly and would expect my auto insurer to pay the bill. I wouldn't want to ignore the dents, nor consider trying to camouflage the damage with a putty filler. So why would I accept anything less when it came to repairing my face?

My job now was to find someone in New Zealand who could actually cut and reposition part of my facial skeleton and put me back together looking hopefully more like my former self. In a country of only four million, finding a surgeon with sufficient experience in such a complex procedure was almost as daunting as the facing the prospect of the procedure itself. When I made enquiries, I was told that my previous surgeon was possibly the only one in New Zealand who might have the experience to do this surgery.

I became a thorn in his side for an entire year after that. Showing him articles from medical journals. Urging him to talk to Dr McCarthy, to let me talk to patients he had performed this type of surgery on, to at least let me see photos. I wanted to know how many times he had done this procedure. He clearly wasn't used to being questioned in this way by a patient. I knew I was alienating him but I understood how specialised and complex this procedure was. I was asking him to refracture my face and put it back together again. I couldn't put my trust in anyone to do that without evidence that they had sufficient experience to actually deliver the goods.

I made it my full-time occupation to get the surgery I had chosen done and to get ACC to pay for it. I wrote to major plastic surgery associations in Australia looking for a surgeon with the skills and experience to perform the surgery there. I wrote to the American surgeon after whom the surgery was named. I studied the ACC law in detail and found a lawyer who offered to take my appeal to court because he agreed with me that the law had provision for payment of overseas surgery when no one in New Zealand could do the job. But I still needed my surgeon's support if there was any possibility of getting the government to pay for my surgery overseas. I needed him to agree with the rationale for the procedure and to say that he had limited experience with that particular procedure. He refused.

By now nearly two years had passed since he had operated on me. I was still ashamed to be seen in public without large sunglasses hiding my face. I felt forced to be dependent on him because of a limited pool of specialist reconstructive plastic surgeons in New Zealand and the ACC legislation restricting payment for overseas surgery. I wrote impotent, angry letters to him that I never sent. Everything I feared about being dependent was playing itself out in my relationship with this surgeon. I was aware that the intensity of my anger and my fear of dependence on him was reminiscent of other frustrating relationships that I had had.

'Transference' is a Freudian term that describes the way in which a patient will sometimes unconsciously ascribe characteristics of and feelings about an important figure in his or her life onto the therapist and play that relationship out in therapy. Sometimes a therapist can unconsciously get caught in the same dynamic. It is a dynamic that can happen in any relationship. In a psychotherapeutic relationship, the therapist is trained to be aware of transference issues when they arise and can use them to help heal an unresolved relationship in the patient's life. But when transference occurs in other types of relationships, for example when a man's relationship with his wife seems to be a replay of his relationship with his mother (or vice versa), it can be destructive. When the emotional dynamic of any relationship feels inappropriately charged it can be helpful to ask yourself, 'Who do they remind me of?' The way that this surgeon responded to my fears and my tears reminded me of my father.

My anger in this situation was not only impotent, it eventually managed to alienate friends. Many wondered why I was more angry about some of my medical experiences than I was about the accident itself. My anger didn't seem reasonable to them. I knew that my anger was a natural and valid part of my grieving process and that none of what had happened to me seemed 'reasonable'. I simply needed to get angry. It was more tolerable than helplessness. But I needed to do it in a way that made me feel less, rather than more helpless.

Anger about the accident itself was the kind of anger that I knew would eat me alive. The accident had happened and nothing I could do would change that. But there was something I could do that might reduce drunk driving and change the laws that failed to adequately address it. It was my anger at the inadequate drunk driving laws that motivated me to do the *60 Minutes* programme. In the same way, it was anger that fuelled my determination to get the surgery I needed with the respect and dignity that I felt I deserved. But that challenge felt insurmountable. Without resolution, my anger ate away at my relationships as well as myself.

No one wants to get dragged down by another into a seemingly bottomless pit with no obvious escape. Most of us respond with 'fight or flight' when threatened. Eventually all but the most saintly of friends and family will back off from or attack chronic anger. While I fought my own demons, some of those around me fled from my anger. I had sufficient 'courage to change the things I could', but not yet the 'serenity to accept the things I couldn't'. And certainly not the 'wisdom to know the difference'! In my journey through grief, I had a long way to go between anger and acceptance. Sometimes that acceptance comes in small spurts and sometimes only from the pure exhaustion of banging your head against the same locked door.

Eventually I made the decision to pursue surgery overseas and to pay for it with my own money if need be. Money I had saved for my retirement. I decided that I'd prefer to spend the money than to be bitter, friendless and disfigured in my old age.

21

Looking for my 'self' in what I do

*I am playing the game of 'if only' with myself again.
If only I could look and feel like me again. If only
I had meaningful work or a relationship or I could
go back 'home' to my family and culture. I don't
know how much difference any of that would really
make. They are at best the futile longings of an ego
in the throes of its own death — a sense of 'me-
ness' trying to survive in a world of separate egos.*

While I fought ACC to cover the cost of surgery overseas
and searched for a surgeon I could trust to restore as
much of my former appearance as was humanly possible, I
found myself back in the limbo of endless waiting. Waiting
for replies to my inquiries from surgeons and surgical
associations. Waiting for a review of my appeal to ACC.
Waiting, I suppose, for rescue. For the comfort of once again

wearing my own face and the hope that that would lead me home to my 'self'. Caught between who I once was and who I would become physically, I remained lost to myself. Without my familiar reflection in the mirror and easy physicality, without a job or family role, I had only my home — a small Victorian cottage filled with items I'd collected over a lifetime — to remind me of who I had been.

My home spoke of a slightly alternative lifestyle. Textiles from around the world hung on the walls. An odd collection of second-hand furniture gave the house a comfortable, warm feeling. Flowers and herbs grew at the back door, and a rickety old shed covered in ivy held the collectables I couldn't fit in the house. I felt safest there, in my own personal space. So much so that as time passed, I began to lose my connection with the outside world as I had done with myself. What I had left were memories. As comforting as they might have been, I knew that they belonged in the past. The longer I hid among my memories, the greater the danger that I would never find out who I was now or even a reason for my hard-earned survival.

So, while I waited for the surgery that I hoped would give me back my face (or something more closely resembling it), I began the search for my 'self' beyond my physical appearance. I decided to look for a new me in what I did, to use my experience to shape a new professional life for myself.

When I was asked by the Corrections Department to talk to groups of repeat driving offenders, I saw an opportunity to create something good out of my experience. I knew that to be heard by them, there could be no room for anger or blame on my part. More than once, I faced a room full of people who, like Jake, had been charged with drunk driving many times and who had continued to drink and drive. Some knew people who had died in drink-driving accidents — friends who had killed themselves and perhaps others because they were driving drunk. None of the group members had ever met a stranger who was a 'victim' of drunk driving. Victims of their actions were always anonymous, and as such, easier to ignore. By meeting them face to face and showing them photos from before the accident of me with family members and friends, I made the consequences of drunk driving more real to them.

I opened with a photo of my mother and myself. 'I am somebody's daughter,' I announced. Then I showed photos of me with my sisters and brothers. 'I am somebody's sister.' Then with nephews. 'I am somebody's auntie.' And then with friends. 'I am somebody's friend.' Then I showed photos of the crumpled cars after the collision followed by a series of photos of me in various stages of recovery in the hospital. Finally, I showed contrasting before and after photos. 'My name is Kathy Torpie and the actions of one drunk driver hurt more people than just me.'

The group participants, some covered in tattoos, listened carefully. I talked to the people that I knew existed behind their tough exteriors. People with mothers, fathers, sisters, brothers, friends, lovers, children. People who hurt to lose friends or family or who lived with the knowledge that they had seriously injured or killed someone. The talks were rich with the sharing of experiences. There was no condemning, just the same opportunity that I had offered to Jake, the opportunity to humanise the consequences of their drunk driving and to acknowledge that they had a choice about whether or not to do it again. From their feedback at the end of the sessions, I left knowing that I got at least some of them thinking differently.

I was encouraged by the response of drunk drivers to my talks, by the success of the *60 Minutes* segment, and by presentations I made to the Victim Support volunteers. But I didn't want to base my new professional identity on my status as a 'victim'. I felt that I had something of value to offer as a psychologist with first-hand experience of the powerful impact that hospital staff can have on their patients' emotional health. I imagined that I could help to change some of the things about the patient/provider relationship in the hospital that I knew could destroy a patient's spirit, even while healing the body. I had tried to communicate some of this to staff while I was still in the hospital and, in a few instances, I think I had some positive effect. But more often than not, my anger at that time alienated those whose view of the provider/patient relationship was so different from my own.

The role of a 'good patient' is typically seen as that of a cooperative, quiet, respectful, compliant, pleasant, undemanding and considerate person. I can see now that, as a frightened and dependent patient, I brought more impotent anger than any of those qualities to my relationships with hospital staff. I was more interested in my own immediate needs than I could possibly have been in the needs of my caregivers under the circumstances. I could no more change their behaviour towards me than a dependent child could change the behaviour of a stressed parent. It was only when I was no longer in the role of a dependent patient that I could respond constructively, with compassion for the plight of both patients and their health care providers, to a relationship that impacts the physical and emotional wellbeing of both.

I attempted to create a position for myself within the hospital system as a consultant and trainer that would use my expertise as a psychologist, together with the many insights that I gained as a hospital patient. I wanted to get involved in the world 'out there' again in a constructive and income-earning way. I spent weeks in the medical school library and on the Internet researching the topic. It became clear to me from my reading that, while there was no conclusive evidence that the relationship between patient and health provider directly influenced the immune system of patients, it did impact on their behaviour and thinking and therefore their clinical outcome. More exciting in terms of the possibility of my getting a 'foot in the door' as a trainer/consultant was research showing that, with improved patient/provider relationships, patient compliance and understanding improved, doctors were able to gather more accurate data and make more accurate diagnoses, and patients were discharged earlier from hospital. It was not only good for patients, it saved money! Excited that I might be able to promote my training in the language of medical administrators intent on saving money, I printed flyers proclaiming 'Resource-full Health Care: Turn Your "Patient Load" Into A Valuable Resource' and mailed them out with an explanation of what improved patient/provider relationships could accomplish. I was on my way, I hoped, to creating a new professional identity as I waited for my new physical identity to take shape.

I soon learned that improved patient/provider relationships would not, in fact, save the hospital money in a socialised health care system. Hospitals in New Zealand were funded according to the population of the area they served rather than the number of patients they actually treated. Although it might be cost-effective on a case-by-case basis, if people spent less time in hospital and more acute surgical patients could be treated, it might actually cost the hospital more money in the long run. I was devastated to be confronted with this kind of thinking by someone within the medical hierarchy. Yet his reasoning made sense — from an economic, if not humanitarian, point of view.

I focused on the fact that New Zealand's socialised health system was moving in the direction of more competitive, market-driven health-care. I approached the new training manager, a manager from the corporate sector who confided that he didn't know much about medicine. At his request, I sent a written proposal, again full of hope that I could use my experience in a positive way while creating a new professional identity for myself. More than a year later, he replied to inform me that his medical colleagues felt it was 'unethical for a patient to train doctors'. Luckily, by now I had at least a bit of the 'wisdom to know the difference' between what I could and couldn't change. I gave up banging my head on that particular locked door. But I never lost my interest in the dynamic between hospital patients and staff and the potential that relationship holds for a healthier health-care system.

Years later, after all my surgeries were over, I attended classes in health psychology in order to learn, in the scientific language of the medical profession, what researchers say about the mind/body connection in health and how the patient/provider relationship fits into that. I learned that the compliant, passive, helpless behaviour commonly expected of a 'good patient' is often related to anxiety, depression and apathy on the part of the patient — none of which is healthy behaviour. The reactive, demanding, critical, sabotaging, and sometimes mutinous behaviour of the 'bad patient' is related to anger and suspicion and can lead the patient to be ignored by staff, to be medicated, prematurely discharged or even referred for psychological intervention. I knew which one I was, and that neither is conducive to healing.

Much is also written about sources of stress for doctors (particularly young training doctors) and nurses in busy hospitals. A study published in the *New Zealand Medical Journal* in 2001 showed that 'More than a third of New Zealand physicians, surgeons, pharmacists and general practitioners have significant symptoms of mental illness' and that '10% had symptoms associated with more "severe" illness' (*New Zealand Herald*, 14 December 2001).

Our health system was indeed sick and in need of attention! Sleep deprivation, economic hardship, staff shortages, maximum case loads, impact on their personal lives, and poor patient outcomes (as well as many other factors) are major sources of stress for those very health professionals who are dealing with frightened, helpless, vulnerable hospital patients every day. Yet, something that seemed to be missing from the literature was the positive effects that improved patient/provider relationships might have on hospital staff as well as on the patients. It is, after all, a relationship.

As a psychologist I had always looked at problems in terms of the context they exist in — the family or business, for example — and how the system itself responded in ways that could actually perpetuate the problem. So, it seemed odd to me that the emotional needs of patients and the emotional needs of the equally human health professionals who care for them are not generally acknowledged as having a powerful influence on each other. The same expectation that puts hospital patients in a passive role, demands an often unrealistic God-like sense of both power and responsibility from their caregivers. It is a dynamic that disables both groups at a time when what they both need most of all is information from each other (good communication), patience with each other, trust in each other to do their part to the best of their ability, and a realistic sense of both the limits and resources that each brings to the relationship.

I imagine that there are doctors and nurses who feel as stressed by unrealistic demands on what they can accomplish within the financial constraints the system imposes upon them as there are patients who feel debilitated by enforced passivity and lack of information. A major tenant of the Hippocratic oath that every doctor must take is to 'cause no harm'. Sadly, it seems to me, that given these constraints the oath is sometimes in conflict with the business of making money.

I continued for some time to try to create a new place for myself in the professional world of training and consultation.

Looking, I suppose, for status and personal validation as much as for an income. I was looking for a credible answer to the inevitable 'What do you do?' so often asked as a social and personal identifier. I was now over fifty and had been out of work long enough to find myself prematurely 'on the shelf'. Like so many others who have found themselves made 'redundant' in the world of work — due to age, illness or economics — when they still have much of value to offer, I felt invisible, invalidated and without status. This was not where I was going to find out who I truly was. I could not rely on work for my identity and value. Anyone who does faces the almost certain prospect of an identity crisis at the end of their working life.

22

Australia

I've been grieving the death of Kathy — not just my appearance and physical limitations — but the Kathy I thought I had neatly defined. I liked her. I loved her. And I miss her terribly. But if Kathy's dead, then who survived? I often find myself retreating from the world 'out there' and going inside to discover (remember?) just who is inhabiting this body. And what a tangle it is! She won't be defined. She knows how ridiculous that is. But she knows too how disorienting it can be to live without the comfort and security (however false it may be) of some constant reference point called 'me'. So I have arranged to go to Australia to have surgery to make the reflection in the mirror look more familiar. Then I can look at it and tell myself, 'Oh! THERE I am!'

I lost the appeal to get the government accident insurance to pay for my surgery overseas ... There was no one in New Zealand I trusted to do it. Either I found someone outside of New Zealand whom I could both afford and trust to do a good job or I accepted living with a physical image that I despised. I knew that beauty is on the inside. That physical beauty fades with time even without an accident. But that didn't help. I wanted to look like me! I hated the stranger in the mirror.

I had been given the name of a prominent surgeon in Australia. His work and credentials seemed impressive, but he was not among those recommended by the various plastic surgery associations of which I had made inquiries. I decided to fly to Australia for an initial consultation and to make up my mind from there.

I arrived at the appointment with the Australian surgeon ready to seriously consider undergoing major facial surgery in a strange country on my own. I was once again prepared with my 'before' photos, my medical records and a long list of questions as well as a large, heavy envelope filled with CAT scans and X-rays. Chairs lined both walls of the waiting room and almost all were filled with people waiting to be seen by the surgeon. As I waited I rehearsed the questions I wanted to be sure to remember to ask and the information I wanted to be sure to let him know. I was nervous. I wanted this to go right. I wanted to leave Australia confident that I had found the right person to do the surgery.

I waited an hour and a half before my name was called. When at last I was brought into the surgeon's office, I was confronted with the largest desk I had ever seen, behind which sat an austere-looking man. He pointed to a seat on the other side of his enormous desk and invited me to sit down. I laid my documents on the desk and reached across the wide expanse between us to shake his hand as I introduced myself. His response was almost comic. Without thinking, he momentarily jerked backward before leaning forward to take my hand. It hadn't occurred to me to be intimidated by the barrier that his desk created between us.

My confidence didn't last long. As I began to carefully explain the history of my injuries, surgeries, and reason for coming all the way from New Zealand to see him, he interrupted.

'Just tell me what you think is wrong with your face.' That was my cue! I reached for my 'before' photos and tried to show him how I once looked and wanted to look again.

'Put those away!' he demanded, sweeping his hand dismissively at the photos that were all I had remaining of my former self. 'That face is gone. I'm not interested in that right now. Tell me about *this* face.'

I couldn't breathe. He might as well have yelled, 'Your child is dead!' or, 'Your marriage is over and that's that! Now let's move on!' I was nowhere near accepting that my face was gone forever. Deflated, I numbly recited the list of things I hoped could be corrected.

'Well, it's flatter and wider and the nose is too short and this cheek is too low and the eyes are uneven and . . .'

He put his hand up several times to slow me down as he typed with two fingers on his computer. Then he looked back at me. 'Anything else?' The worst of my symptoms had yet to be spoken.

'The last surgeon filled my face with some kind of artificial material because there wasn't enough bone. Now whenever I smile it feels like a grimace. It's awful! My face doesn't just look different. It feels different!'

Until my last surgery, I had never realised that a face is more than a vehicle to express oneself in the world. It is a vital feedback mechanism that, through muscle and nerves working together, gives the physical sensation inwardly of whatever your face is expressing outwardly. Smile. It feels good! Now frown, or grimace or scrunch up your eyebrows ... Each feels different. I had lost the sense of congruence not only between who I believed myself to be and the image I saw in the mirror, but also between what I felt internally and the messages my facial expressions fed back to me. Every time I laughed, the message to my brain was that something was wrong.

'That's psychological,' he replied. 'I can't fix that.'

He didn't understand. I panicked.

'No! No! I mean it doesn't feel, you know physically *feel* like a smile and I . . .'

'Of course it doesn't! Women have facelifts and don't feel like themselves for a year.'

I wanted to run out of the room. Instead I began to cry.

'You're very anxious, I can see,' he said. 'You must understand that I can't spend more than an hour with any one patient.'

I snivelled 'Yes,' and snuck a look at my watch. I'd been in his office for fifteen minutes.

'I can't answer every minutia, every small detail. You can get away with that in the States, but they'll charge you a fortune. Here you just risk getting on people's wrong side.'

That was it. I felt myself crumble. I had put so much hope (and money) into this consultation. Whatever he said after that seemed to go right past me, covered over by the loud static of my fear and disappointment. The surgeon stood when it was time for me to leave.

I stood up and shook his hand in the end and we left his office to arrange dates for surgery. Where else could I go? He let some compassion — or was it pity? — show. 'You poor thing. You really are so anxious.'

I returned to New Zealand all but defeated. Tired of trying so hard to make headway and seemingly getting nowhere. I felt worn down by the decisions I faced alone and by the barriers I seemed to find everywhere. It had taken me more than a year to finally decide to go to Australia to be assessed by this one particular surgeon. I had found someone capable of doing the surgery, but I felt intimidated. Could I possibly go alone to another country, where I knew no one, to have this surgeon peel the skin from my face then saw and reposition bones before putting me back together? Could I survive alone for six weeks while I recovered, in a strange country after a surgery like that? Was I that brave? I was torn between sides of myself that I knew well and those that were new to me — the weak and the tough, the fearful and brave, the dependent and the self-reliant. They were all parts of me and all had to be given an equal voice in this decision. Otherwise, I knew, I would betray some part of myself no matter what decision I made.

ACC sent me to see a plastic surgeon in Wellington, New Zealand's capital city. When I presented him with my long list of things I wanted corrected, he asked me to pick the three most important. He gently explained that it probably wasn't possible to accomplish all that I hoped for. I struggled with having to limit my hopes to just three things. But I was clear that the position of my cheekbone and eye were certainly high on my list of priorities. The operation I wanted to reposition my cheekbone was complex, he warned, and suggested bone grafts instead. Again I compared my face to a damaged car packed with filler to cover up, rather than repair, the damage. I wanted better than that. But, I confessed, I was terrified of making myself physically and emotionally vulnerable in Australia, so far from the support of friends and family.

He explained that the surgery I wanted was not something that was often called for in a small country like New Zealand and that he did not have experience with that particular procedure to do it himself. He told me of an Oxford-trained plastic surgeon in Australia with an excellent reputation who was certainly capable of doing the surgery. This surgeon was soon to be in New Zealand to train some local surgeons and, if he agreed to perform the surgery on me while he was in New Zealand, the Wellington surgeon would 'move heaven and earth' to see that ACC paid for it. To organise that, I would have to travel once again to Australia at my own expense for a consultation. I jumped at the chance! Imagining that I could have the surgery I so desperately wanted performed by a well-known, highly experienced plastic surgeon, have it paid for by ACC — and be able to recover at home with the support of friends . . . I felt the worst of the struggle was all but over. I wanted to hug the plastic surgeon. I felt taken care of in a way that I desperately needed. That care transformed my defeat into deep gratitude and renewed hope. All would be well!

In the years of searching for a way to get my face back, I discovered that hope isn't always a positive thing. Whether it proves to be friend or foe is often a matter of time. Endless, unanswered hope can be a form of slow torture. Like fear, hope is always about something that might happen in the future. It is never about what is right here and now. If whatever we fear actually comes to pass, it often comes with the relief of not having to live in fear of that thing one moment longer, regardless of the other consequences. I discovered that the same can be true of hope. Like fear, hope can remove us from the present and leave us hanging somewhere between what is and what might be. When what is happening in the present is unbearable, hope can motivate us to do all we possibly can to shape the outcome that we hope for as we wait for the future to unfold. But when the waiting itself becomes unbearable and passive, even a disappointing outcome can be a relief. It's only after whatever you fear or hope for actually comes to pass (or not) that you can begin to deal with it and move forward. There is a difference, I found, between taking refuge in the hope that present circumstances can be changed and in allowing hope to keep you from knowing that this is one of those things you cannot change. Without recognising the difference, depression is more likely than the serenity of knowing and coming to accept that this loss, no matter how terrible, is final.

The Oxford-trained surgeon refused to do more than

bone grafts to fill the bony asymmetries of my face. There wasn't going to be any rescue from my dilemma. No 'perfect' solution on offer. I had a choice to make. Free bone grafting by a highly competent surgeon on my home turf or spend many thousands of dollars to have far more complex surgery in another country where my only support would be from kind strangers. No one could make the decision for me. It was time to bite the bullet.

23

New face — final surgery

This surgery is going to be brutal and the results unknown. Am I really willing to allow myself to undergo physical, emotional and financial hardship so that my face, my image, will be more pleasing, more safely familiar? So that I can defy what happened to me? So that I can overcome adversity and emerge victorious?

My mind was like a debating chamber, constantly weighing the pros and cons. What was left of the control freak in me came roaring to the forefront. I should accept no halfway measures, it insisted. It would be hard, but I would survive. In the end I would know that I had done all I possibly could do. Imagine being disappointed with the outcome of bone grafts and having always to wonder, 'What if . . . ?' In the background, the exhausted, vulnerable side of myself begged for mercy. A deal was struck. Just this one more try. Then no more, I promised myself. Just stay strong a little bit longer.

It was 1997, three and a half years since the accident. During that time a friend from the States had come to visit and stayed. She was living what felt like a rerun of the magical life I led when I first came to New Zealand in the seventies. She had fallen in love with New Zealand and was living an alternative lifestyle on an island three hours from the city. I had just visited there for several days, glad to have her in my life on this side of the world. She reminded me of who I once was — adventurous and brave — just as I was about to embark on my journey to Australia in search of a more familiar reflection of that self. The morning that I was to fly to the States for a family visit before heading to Australia for my surgery, I woke to a radio news broadcast. My friend had gone missing from her isolated little house near the sea. I postponed my trip for three days in a row, waiting for word that she had been found. There was a huge police investigation and search for her. She was never found. Nancy's adventurous free-spirited life came to an abrupt halt as quickly and unexpectedly as my own. Only she was presumed dead and I wasn't. It was under this heavy cloud that I set off for my final surgery.

I had already spoken at length with the surgeon's nurse about arrangements for my hospital stay and recovery. A hospital social worker was assigned to be my official support person. She arranged for me to stay free of charge for six weeks during my recovery in the nurses' residence attached to the hospital. I could get my meals in the hospital cafeteria. There would be other overseas patients living there, as well as out-of-town family members of patients. My friend's sister and her husband lived nearby and offered to support me while I was there. A friend elsewhere in Australia rallied a local friend of hers to send and receive emails for me so that I could keep in touch with family and friends. The social worker would send a car to meet me at the airport. A week of appointments had been scheduled with specialists who were part of the surgery team approach. All was in order. The controlling (read fearful) part of my self was well satisfied that my needs would be well looked after. My fear began to feel more like excitement as the time drew near. On the flight from the States to Australia, I happened to sit next to attractive single man who asked to see me again. It didn't miss my notice how ironic that was. Here I was headed to have major facial surgery, yet my spirited optimism was having a stronger impression on him than my physical image!

I phoned the surgeon's office when I got to Australia. I had already received an itinerary of pre-surgery appointments with medical specialists that were part of the plastic surgeon's 'team approach'. Only after being assessed for surgery by each of these specialists, would I be seen by the plastic surgeon. Then a team meeting would be held between the plastic surgeon, other members of the team and myself. I had chosen this plastic surgeon, in part, for the confidence that his team approach (and my inclusion in it) gave me. But, when I arrived for my scheduled appointments with a private physician, a neurologist, and an eye surgeon, not one of them knew what I was there for! The receptionist had sent referrals without sufficient information about me, the surgery, or what information the plastic surgeon required of them.

No one had seen my X-rays or CAT scans. I was furious, and less confident by the minute. Not one of the 'team' had even been notified that there was to be a team consultation held on Friday afternoon in preparation for my surgery on Monday morning! The only member of the 'team' to arrive was the one that I had personally mentioned the consultation to and whom I asked to attend. As far as I was concerned, my long-awaited surgery was being compromised by an inexperienced receptionist. I couldn't believe it. But there was no turning back now. I had already paid a $10,000 deposit. And I knew that if I backed out now I would never again find the courage to pursue such major surgery again.

By the time I arrived for my consultation with the plastic surgeon at the end of the week I was panicked. I was afraid that I was exactly the kind of patient that this particular surgeon would have little patience for. I felt utterly vulnerable and alone. I asked the hospital social worker to come to the appointment with me as a support person. As I complained to him that team approach was not working and I felt my care was being seriously compromised, he kept glancing at the social worker. She patted my knee. It was intended to calm me, I know, but it felt more like a warning. 'Don't,' she seemed to be saying. The surgeon insisted that he ask the questions, not me. I knew of his reputation. He was a good surgeon. But I was frightened of him emotionally and that was enough to make me doubt that he cared as much about what I wanted as what he thought I needed.

The dynamic between us would have been amusing to most observers. The surgeon and I were not unlike two rivalling siblings fighting it out in front of 'Mom'.

Me: Can you correct the sunkenness beneath my right eye?

Him: There's nothing wrong with that eye.

Me: There is! It sits further back in my head. Even my family comments that it looks artificial. It feels artificial!

Him: It looks fine to me.

Me: You told me that you agreed with Dr McCarthy's assessment. (I hand him the referral letter I'd brought last time.)

Him: If Dr McCarthy can make that eye better then by all means go to him.

It was at that point that the social worker patted my knee and reminded me that I'd had a terrible accident. This was my face and I needed to be included in the decision-making. I had to know that we were on the same track. I took notes of what the surgeon said and asked him to confirm that I understood correctly exactly what he was going to do. Dr McCarthy's assessment had referred to the fact that I had bilateral enopthalmos — that both eyes were positioned incorrectly in my facial skeleton — and my reflection in the mirror told me that was true. Now, at the eleventh hour, this surgeon decided that I did not have enopthalmos on the right side. He would leave the right side of my face completely untouched. He did, however, agree to everything else, which by then I considered a victory. This was one of those times when I had the wisdom to know the difference between what I could change and what I could not.

I checked into the hospital on the Monday morning and was asked to pay in advance. Then I was shown to a large double room with only one bed. That seemed luxurious to me. I was told that I would be recovering in an intensive care unit the first few days following the surgery. The price (I was paying for this myself) was shocking. So, when the anaesthetist came for his pre-op visit I asked if being in the intensive care unit was really necessary. He said it wasn't and that he'd arrange to have me recover in my private room instead.

The morning after surgery, I woke to the sound of jack-hammers — yes, jackhammers! — on the outside wall of my hospital room. They were doing renovations! With facial bones newly fractured and held together with metal screws, the pain was devastating. I begged to be moved but was told that there were no available rooms. I was taken in a wheelchair to the lobby but it was being painted and the smell overwhelmed me so soon after anaesthesia. A kind nurse discovered me later outside, huddled in my wheelchair in the hot Australian sun. It was 42°C, hotter than anything I had ever experienced, but better by far than the jackhammers. This sweet angel of mercy got angry on my behalf and found me a room away from the noise where I fell gratefully into the soothing relief of cool sheets, soft pillows and much needed sleep. By the time I woke again there were many messages for me from friends and family on three continents. I even got a call from the man I met on the plane. The social worker visited on her day off. The surgeon's office nurse phoned and invited me to a day out with her when I had sufficiently recovered. My friend's sister Kathryn and her husband Jürgen invited me to stay with them when I was well enough. There were emails and flowers. I wasn't alone after all. Not one bit!

I was there for six weeks recovering in my ten-by-twelve-foot cement-block room in the nurses' residence. The one window looked out over the botanical gardens. Before the surgery I had transformed the room into a temporary 'home' with music and a few familiar items that I brought with me. With the fan smuggled in for me by a compassionate maintenance man, I was comfortable and secure in my tiny abode while I waited for the results of the surgery to reveal themselves. I was, of course, hideous-looking. Swollen and distorted, the whites of my eyes blood red, staples in my head and sutures beneath my eyes and behind my ears. But I soon encountered some of the others living on my hall who were also plastic surgery patients. I became friendly with a young woman who had been born with a purple growth on her face that continued to grow until it covered more than half of her face. She had a fist-sized lump protruding from her forehead where the surgeon had inserted a balloon, gradually blowing it up, to stretch her non-discoloured skin. He was going to surgically remove the excess skin and graft it over the discoloured parts of her face. I had waited three years for my surgery. She had waited a lifetime.

The kindness and generosity that I experienced amazed and delighted me. These were strangers who had taken me under their wing, who had invited me into their homes, had visited me on their days off, taken me out, or come at night to visit. Most especially I could not have coped as I did without the incredible kindness and generosity of spirit of Kathryn and Jürgen, who became my surrogate family in Australia. Once I was well enough, they invited me not only into their home, but into their lives. We shared Christmas together shortly before I left Australia. And when I returned eight months later for follow-up surgery, they took me into their home once again.

In the nurses' residence I lived side by side with people the likes of which I had never before met and probably never would have, had it not been for the circumstances that brought us together. I met people from the Australian outback who lived miles from any neighbours. Their skin like toughened hides from the Australian sun, these were hard-working, hard-playing individuals. I made friends with a man in his forties who had been living on the streets for years. Years ago he had been in a motorcycle accident and the skin of his face had been torn away by the rough gravel on the road. His entire jaw was built of titanium and every tooth in his mouth was man-made. He too had a rough exterior. I would have been afraid of him had I encountered him on a dark street alone at night. But he had a gentle heart. He befriended an old Aboriginal man from the Northern Territory who had just been diagnosed with a terminal disease. They got drunk together on cheap wine in the room next to mine. When I heard the diagnosis, I joined them in a drink, though it was strictly forbidden (and not the best thing to do only a few weeks after surgery). There was an odd bond between us that went beyond the lives we led in the world beyond those walls. One of the things about shared loss is that it so often becomes an equaliser, one that discards the barriers and demarcations that normally separate us at a time when we most need connection. When you're in the trenches together, it doesn't matter where you come from. Any soldier can tell you that. So can any hospital patient.

I was aware that everyone at home would be anxious to see the results of this long-awaited surgery. I wanted to feel triumphant. 'Tra La! Kathy's back!' I wanted to thrill and delight friends with some dramatic physical transformation. To 'wow!' them. But I knew that, although there was a definite improvement, Kathy was not back and probably never really would be. The much-anticipated thrill of victory simply wasn't there, just an aching exhaustion. I was fearful, too, of pity. 'Poor Kathy. Was it worth it?' But there was only love and support when I returned. The most memorable highlight of my time in Australia was not the outcome of my surgery — there was more to be done — but the flood of love and support that I had pretty much the entire time I was there. The best part was not the feeling of victory, but of gratitude.

I returned to New Zealand at the beginning of the New Year. It was 1998. The year after my accident I had made a resolution to myself that every day would include time for physical activity, for creative expression, for being a friend or lover and for silence. I had progressed from physiotherapy to t'ai chi and yoga, had done a bit of writing (especially in my journal) and maintained those relationships that I could. The time for silence was easy. This year I decided it was time for new resolutions. Time to be really conscious of wearing masks for the comfort of others and for my own security. I had always been most comfortable, most relaxed, in my own company. I loved being 'on stage', loved the attention and occasional applause. But it was off-stage that I let out a sigh of relief. Too often the relief would dissolve into emptiness when the eyes reflected at me in the mirror would challenge, 'Now what?', as if, without the audience and the recognition, I was insubstantial.

I was determined this year to get off-stage more often, even when I was with others, to be the audience more often, to applaud more loudly and more often. Life is, after all, a drama, I reasoned. Why not live as though I knew it was only a drama, whether I'm playing audience or am on centre stage. I could learn to improvise my role, engaged in life's drama without being tied down to a 'script'. I was looking for a new 'me' without being restricted to a narrow role seeking the limelight. I found it hard. Everywhere people wanted to define me by what I did. 'What do you do?', 'What have you been doing lately?', 'What are you doing this weekend?' Every time I was asked those questions, I felt as though I was being asked to justify my life. I felt forced into the limelight in a way that I hated. Because the answer was so often, 'Nothing.' I felt like I was being asked to admit that I was nothing. That there was no justification for my life. Every time that I had to admit that I don't do anything, I felt ashamed. Every time that I tried to fill my life with activity for the sake of belonging, I felt even more ashamed. In the end, staying at home on my own was as close as I could get to getting off-stage. I'd always felt like a bit of an outsider. Instead of coping with that by standing out, as I usually did, I went into hiding.

The results of surgery were good, but some corrections still needed to be made. I returned to Australia nine months later for 'touch-up' surgery. On the day of the surgery the nurse presented me with the consent form agreeing to what I understood the surgeon was going to do. It left out something he had said he would do. He had put fat into my eyelid the last time and it didn't work. It looked like, well, a lump of fat in my eyelid. He had agreed to remove it, but it was not on the list. So I waited to talk to him before signing the consent form. Every surgery I had ever had included a pre-surgery bedside visit.

The surgeon never came. As I lay on the gurney just outside the doors of the operating room waiting for his arrival, he came up to me, holding the unsigned consent form. I was afraid he was angry that I hadn't signed it. He had changed his mind about doing my eyelid and didn't have time to discuss it. I should trust his judgement on this. It wasn't his judgement I was worried about. If I didn't believe that he was a good surgeon I would never have put myself in his hands. It was the way I felt he was relating to me that concerned me. I was really scared! This man was about to cut me open again with a scalpel. I backed down, tried to calm his anger and signed the paper. Then they wheeled me in, put me under and the surgeon took up his scalpel.

I woke in the recovery room whimpering, then sobbing. Somehow the anaesthetic removed my armour. The nurse asked if I was in pain and all I could say was, 'I'm so sad.' I was sad for Kathy, as though she were my precious child rather than my self. She'd been through so much. I felt little and lonely . . . and in some strange way, abused. I had handed myself over to a surgeon who had just yelled at me! I had submitted utterly to his power. It felt like a violation of trust somehow (though he did nothing to physically harm me). Once again, I wanted my Mommie. I had the same response to finding myself in this strange place all alone and in pain as I might have if I really was only a small child. A deep sadness came over me. A breathless, vast pause. So deep that the only way I could give it a name was from the tears that I felt rolling down my cheeks. I also felt old. Now that I had finally come to the end of my surgeries, the armour that had been so heavy to bear — yet so essential to my ability to keep trying, to keep waiting, to keep believing — began to crumble. At last, I didn't have to be strong any more!

A month or so later I saw my surgeon for my final follow-up visit. I looked better by far, but there was one thing more that I needed to accomplish before I left. This surgeon had made it possible for me to see some reflection of the person I remembered in the mirror, to look in the mirror without feeling repulsed or ashamed by what I saw. But in the process I felt emotionally battered. I needed to be met by him with the respect and compassion that I knew was essential to my healing and that, until now, felt totally lacking.

I brought the social worker with me because I felt I needed her support. He didn't like being questioned and I had some questions for him that I wanted answered. I had it rehearsed in my mind. I began with thanks for all the improvements he had made before asking why he hadn't done some of the things he promised and why my cheek and temple were now so hollow. He cut me off.

'You, of all people, should know that the final results won't be apparent for six months to a year. You don't like the results one month after surgery! That's unbelievable! Really unbelievable!' He looked to the social worker as if to say, 'Do you see now what I have to put up with?'

I told him that I knew enough to know that swelling goes down in time but that hollows don't fill in and my cheek and temple were now hollow.

'You have this pattern,' he said. 'You come in with a long

list of questions and after I spend hours answering them in great detail, you present me with the same questions at the door of the theatre.' His voice was rising and he was appealing to the social worker with repeated glances in her direction.

I held fast. There was nothing to lose any more. I didn't have to be frightened or conciliatory. I told him that I wasn't sure if it was a good idea to have the social worker present since he seemed to be directing more energy toward defending himself to her than to communicating with me.

'You're right,' I said. 'I do have a pattern. It goes like this. I ask questions and take notes. Then I check your notes to see if you actually heard my concerns and if we have the same understanding about what you are going to do. I wanted confirmation that you indeed intended to do what you said. That's why I asked again. Please don't make me fight you for my rights as a patient to be informed and involved in my own care.'

Then I took a giant leap. 'I'm going to take a risk here,' I said. 'I know that you don't want to get personally involved with your patients. But like it or not what you do to patients is extraordinarily personal. You remove my skin, enter my body and do things that will affect me every day for the rest of my life. You have my face in your hands! The part of me that gives others the first impression of who I am.'

He threw his hands in the air. 'That's the worst bunch of rubbish I have ever heard!'

I was stunned. Quietly I replied, 'Don't patronise me. I am an intelligent adult just like you.'

He began to reply, then stopped.

'OK, that was patronising, but . . .' Something changed then. He looked to the social worker and then back to me. Explaining that this was not his forte, he gently, compassionately urged me to move forward with my life and stop training friends to see the defects in my face. I asked if he had any idea what it took for me to face surgery sixteen times, any idea what I had to make him in my mind in order to allow him to refracture my face and reposition my bones.

'No,' he almost whispered, 'I can hardly imagine it even once. I could keep going, Kathy, but it would only hurt you. Enough is enough. I've done the best that I can. I wish I could make it better, but I can't.'

I mumbled that it was hope that I had to let go of.

'Yes,' he said, 'that too.'

I knew in that instant that letting go of the hope would present me with the losses that I had yet to grieve. All this time I had held grief at bay because grief shut the door on hope. Finally, after sixteen surgeries, I knew that continued hope would be more unbearable than loss. As I said my goodbyes, I told the surgeon that I hadn't wanted to hear what he had to say but that I finally could because he had found a way to say it so that I was able to hear it.

'I appreciate it,' I said as I shook his hand. 'I suspect that this was even more difficult for you than the surgery.' He smiled warmly and nodded.

'You got that right.'

24

Looking for my self
in a relationship

Genuine single male seeks female. Slim, athletic . . .

A few years after the completion of my reconstructive
surgery in Australia, a New Zealand plastic surgeon did
the remaining touch-ups I needed. With fat injections and
some grafts of fat and rib cartilage, he filled the remaining
hollows and asymmetries of my face. With all of the final
touch-up surgeries to my face finally completed, I was finally
looking normal. No more of what I called my 'Picasso' look. No
more obvious asymmetries. In fact I was looking a lot like my
old self. It was a relief no longer to feel alienated by the image
in the mirror. The image I saw was more attractive and more
familiar. But it was an image, and I knew it. The mirror was not
where I was going to find the sense of self that I had lost.

I think much of my renewed feeling of attractiveness came from my plastic surgeon's manner as much as from his surgical skills. He treated me with the gentleness that I had craved throughout my recovery. By doing so, he of all my surgeons healed wounds so deep that no scalpel could reach them. He made me feel like an attractive, intelligent, courageous and worthwhile human being. Not a set of clinical challenges, or something broken and in need of repair. Somehow he managed to make all of our clinical visits feel personal as well as clinical. He came out to greet me personally at every appointment, as he did for every patient, always with a warm smile. I felt like I was in the hands of a friend whom I could trust completely, someone who acknowledged the person behind the remaining facial flaws as well as the flaws themselves. He must have known that for the beauty within to reveal itself, it needs to be acknowledged. He took an interest in what I thought and felt, in a way that humanised the doctor/patient relationship without compromising it. I felt in every way personally acknowledged and included in my care. He was a true healer in every sense of the word.

Because he saw more than my pathology and reflected that in the way he dealt with me, I was encouraged to begin to look at myself in the same way. I confess that I had something of a crush on him. It is an embarrassing cliché, I know, but each time I saw him I came away feeling special. I saw no photos in his office of wife and family. No ring on his left hand. I let my imagination make me special in his eyes, although I saw that he was kind and gentle to all of his patients. The image I had always had of my perfect man was tall and rugged, clad in jeans. The Marlboro man — without the cigarette. The physical opposite of my surgeon. I smile now to realise what a gift it was to find myself attracted to someone so physically different from the image I previously held as my ideal. It was his gentleness, kindness and intelligence that attracted me. I thought he was wonderful — bow tie and all!

During one procedure, as he suctioned fat from my belly to fill in the contours of my face, and his nurse assisted, I asked if he had any children. He had made some small joke or teasing comment as the fat came squelching from my belly into the syringe. The kind of thing I imagine one would say to make a child laugh. I thought he'd be a wonderful father. Gentle, reassuring, teasing. He could make me at ease even as he sucked fat from my belly! Yes, he replied. He had two. Then he told a little story about asking his son one day how he'd feel if Mommie and Daddy didn't live together any more. Was he trying to tell me something? He was, but not what I thought. He went on to say he was only teasing. 'Mommie and I love each other very much' he reassured his son . . . And me.

He knew! He knew I had a crush on him and he was taking this opportunity to set me straight without embarrassing me, without my losing face. The crush came to an end as soon as I knew he was married. But my respect and gratitude grew. And I still felt attractive! Enough so that I began to believe it might be possible that someone more available might see it. I started checking out the Internet personal ads as a testing ground for a relationship. For the first time in years I felt gutsy and confident as a woman ready for a relationship with someone special. Maybe the new me was to be found in 'we'.

One day while going through my emails, I noticed the link to personals on my browser. 'Over here!' it seemed to say. 'Check this out.' So I did. I clicked on, surfed around, and there he was, almost at the top of the list!

Wouldn't it be great if you could simply be standing in an elevator waiting to go to the seventy-first floor when suddenly the door opens on the fourth floor and in walks someone ... not just anyone, but SOMEONE. Your eyes meet, turn away in a moment of shyness, and return with the full realisation that in the initial moment, you both understood something about each other ... a genuine mutuality ... a chemistry that neither of you could deny. He asks you to please press the sixtieth floor and something begins that you both somehow know will continue into the future. Well, this hasn't happened to me yet — not quite like that but it's a nice fantasy nevertheless. Perhaps I should spend more time in elevators, but who has the time? Which is why I'm sending this out to you. I spend so much of my time in a world of focused creativity, that I just don't have time for elevators and singles bars don't interest me. I'd love to experience a connection with the kind of chemistry I just spoke of, it would be so nice ... I'm a healthy, sincere, educated and passionate person. I'm awed by life's surprises and still quite adventurous (most of the time). I'd like to meet the woman in the elevator who, like me, doesn't have extra time to ride them but believes that such things can happen. If this strikes

a chord in you (and it probably does or you wouldn't
have read this far), get back to me. (Prefer women
35–46, 5'1"–5'8", slim/slender to average weight.)

'Who is this man?' I wondered. It seemed almost as
random a 'meeting' as the elevator encounter he had
described. I imagined someone open, gentle and intelligent
with a creative streak and sense of humour. Someone so
interesting that I simply had to answer! His ad stood out to
me because, unlike the others, it sounded like the beginning
of a conversation rather than an interview. I wanted to
continue that conversation!

So, the elevator reaches the sixtieth floor and the
doors open. Do both exit together? Does one get off?
Or do both remain as the doors close again? What
about the appointments they're headed toward? The
doors are about to close! What would YOU do?

I felt a bit giddy as I waited for his reply, which came the
same day.

Easy question — what would I do as the elevator
reaches our respective floors? If I had followed my
heart in the past perhaps I wouldn't be looking for
a soul mate right now. To hell with the meetings or
appointments, sometimes love is more important. A
'yes' or a 'no' is so much better than a 'maybe' or a
'what if?'. What would you do? And by the way, let's
share a little more about each other now because

maybe the search engine will crash tonight and our connection will be forever lost!

This was it! Mr Right! He'd also written a second ad, which was more of a shopping list for 'everything I am looking for', but one with spark and humour. I read his ad to my best friend who replied 'My God! He talks just like you! This guy sounds perfect for you!' I had to tell myself to slow down a bit. Step by step. Just reply. Don't be rushed by some imaginary fear that the search engine will crash. Deep breath. Be honest. Just continue the conversation.

How would I respond? Hmmm? If I was headed to the seventy-first floor and you didn't move to get off when the doors opened on sixty, I'd smile and tell you how glad I was that you did that. If you did step off, I'd like to think that I'd step off with you and, when the doors closed behind us, ask 'What did you do THAT for?' But I'm not sure. I might convince myself that I was just imagining the chemistry. You want to know more about me. What do you want to know? Height? Weight? Profession? Age? Am I 'everything you're looking for?' I'm not applying for a job. Neither are you. Can you REALLY take a risk? Talk to me! I've read your wish-list. I don't think you'd be disappointed.

I didn't want our conversation to turn into an interview, an application for love.

He replied right away. Only he sounded different this

time. Impatient. He wondered if I was 'playing games' and if perhaps I wanted to remain 'mysterious' a little longer. A real 'let's get down to it' type of guy. He wanted a resumé of my qualities as well as a photo, and pretty much right now!

I find games at this stage off-putting because my time is valuable.

I should have stopped right there. 'Mr Right' wasn't going to turn out to be so perfect after all. But, I turned a blind eye and reasoned that if we had met on an elevator there wouldn't be much time for either of us to make the kinds of decisions one does when considering pursuing a potential relationship. I wanted him to be the person I imagined him to be from his ad. He had already shown himself to be so much of what I really like in a man that I ignored any evidence to the contrary. So I gave him what he wanted, my description. The whole shebang: height, weight, age, profession and personal qualities. The photo could be arranged too. I felt like I was being asked to take my clothes off — to expose myself — a little too quickly. He wanted a woman five to fifteen years younger than himself (I'm three years older than him) and was hoping to find his perfect woman living in a nearby suburb (I didn't). I thought for sure that my age and location would put him off, but decided to risk revealing all.

. . . If you would be willing to take a risk with that 'someone' on the elevator, you might want to continue the conversation we've begun. It could be that the

different relationship we each have with time is too
big a barrier, or that I live so far away. I guess I'll leave
that to you to decide.

The reply was warm, gentle and welcoming. My age
didn't seem to be an issue or even that I lived so far away.
He revealed more about himself and asked me to write him a
'long, long letter', which I did. A letter that exposed some of
the things about me that lay beneath the surface I'd already
given him. Instead of hitting him with both barrels, with
stories of some of the unusual and exciting things that I've
done with my life that so far have never failed to win me
interest if not admiration, I told him about the very normal
part of myself that he would surely get to meet if ever we
were in a long-term relationship. The things you usually try to
hide when making first impressions. That I sometimes liked to
blob in front of the television with a bowl of ice cream, or that
I could be happily entertained for hours writing, gardening,
or simply watching the birds in my garden play tug-of-war
with the worms. We'd been writing a couple of times a day
by now. I figured that it was probably better to hit him with
the boring, everyday part of me first rather than try to make
a great first impression to hide behind. He didn't write back.
For three days he didn't write back! Three long days in which
I felt myself put my barriers back in place. Finally I hunted
down his newly edited ad back in the Personals, pretty much
the same elevator ad and I clicked on 'reply'.

. . . The elevator reaches the sixtieth floor. The doors
open. He invites you to continue the conversation

you've begun. You decide to take the risk and you
step off the elevator with him. As the elevator doors
close behind you, you turn to him and . . . he walks
away!

Then he was back! He said it was a computer glitch, that
he never got my long letter. He included photos of himself
and his kids. He was short, not particularly physically
attractive and I imagined that his large hat was covering a
bald head. But that wasn't the important thing. He sounded
funny and intelligent, if a bit impatient. I re-sent my long
letter and some photos. But I felt wary. There wasn't the
same kind of excitement. A new kind of 'Who is this man . . .
really?' had crept into my mind. But a friendly reply came the
next morning acknowledging receiving my letter and photos
and promising to write at the end of the day. All was well! It
was in that frame of mind that I looked forward to his reply
that night. I clicked on before going to bed and there on the
screen before me appeared a letter that must surely have
been written by a different person! With the formal brevity of
a notice of non-acceptance for a job application, he informed
me that I didn't get the job!

I want to thank you for taking the time to write to me
and sending me the pictures. It has been interesting
sharing thoughts/stories but my feeling is that we
probably aren't going to have a romantic connection.
If you want to continue to correspond anyway that
would be fine.

Stunned, I stared at the computer screen reading his words over and over. It wasn't just the rejection, though that was certainly bad enough after revealing so much of myself. It was the utter inconsistency between the image I had of the man who had written the ad — gentle, humorous, open, creative, intelligent — and the author of this abrupt, rather cool, patronising letter. This utter stranger somehow managed to undermine my tentative sense of myself as an attractive woman.

I continued to read personal ads every now and then, but knowing that even the 'perfect ad' is just another version of the perfect first impression, scripted and edited for approval. I guess finding love will always come down to the old-fashioned, time-consuming ritual of exposing layer upon layer to find the true heart and soul of another person.

It was a long time before I answered an ad. Another American. We spoke for a few hours on the phone and seemed to have an easy connection. He was a widower and shared the story of his wife's tragic illness and death. I told him about the accident. Each of us had had a life-transforming experience involving immense loss. It felt safe to send him my photo after such an intimate conversation. It wasn't. But by now I knew that there was far more of me to know and love than my physical image.

> . . . I appreciate you sending the photo — thanks for finding one. You have asked me to be honest, and whether or not you asked me to be so, I would be. As I mentioned some time ago I'm a visual person and photos tell me a lot about a person and my attraction

to them. From the little that we have written and talked on the phone, you have impressed me as a person that I would like to get to know better. If the photo is a fair representation, I feel that I would not be as drawn to you physically as much as I have been mentally and spiritually. I know this is a human frailty or weakness that I have, i.e., I put too much emphasis on physical attraction — it is something I've realised for some time that I need to work on. While I feel that we could become good friends given the chance, I don't feel the relationship possibilities, at least at this point in time, are there . . .

Admittedly, I have my own preferences about appearances. We all do. But I have learned that I don't want to get close to anyone who values my physical appearance above the rest of who I am. I already spent years doing that to myself.

I just got your email. Well, not 'just'. I gave myself a few minutes to take it in before responding . . . Thank you for your honesty. I don't imagine it is easy to be honest and up-front when it comes to telling someone you're not attracted to them. It's certainly not easy to hear — but that's my stuff.

Since my accident, the issue of 'face' has been both central in my life and confusing. I know my 'self' far better than I ever did before I woke up one day without the face I had always thought of as 'me'. Almost as soon as I realised that who I am goes far beyond my personality or appearance, I was desperate to get my face back. To 're-cover'. Though I stopped thinking of my face as 'me', I knew I lived in a world where others have nothing else to go on when they first meet you and might sometimes never get beyond appearances. So I understand. This face is the best they could do and I am grateful for it. It's not beautiful, but it's a miracle. I was prettier before but, I figure that just like everyone else, my appearance was destined to change with age anyway.

I feel a bit like I lost a security blanket with my attractiveness. But I feel like a better person in many ways than the person I was before the accident. The time I took just now before responding to you was time I needed to check in with the me on the inside. She's OK. She's fine! Disappointed, but fine . . .

I am still single and that's OK. Relationships aren't meant to be carefully composed and edited as they can be on the Internet. Thinking that I might find my 'self' by finding 'Mr Right' was a mistake that lots of people make. It's a mistake that can trap both partners behind the perfect images they presented and fell in love with, leaving no room for either to grow. Without a good sense of who 'I' am and the freedom to be that person, saying 'i love you' can be more of a plea for love than a gift of one's self. Love is a tricky business no matter how you approach it.

25

Emotional wounds

I had anticipated that the end of my surgeries would be a time for celebration. That I would feel victorious. Liberated. And once again, invincible. But that is not to be. What I feel is exhausted. Utterly spent.

For five years I had held grief at bay in my resolve to overcome what had happened to me. I had been in an almost constant state of anger, fear, and determination, fighting to get my life back. But I had failed to recognise the emotional cost of my physical recovery. In order to face surgery, and all that entailed, so many times, I had remained emotionally shut down to the frightened, lonely, vulnerable person that I had discovered as I lay bleeding and waiting for rescue on an isolated country road five years earlier.

She re-emerged almost immediately after my final surgery

in Australia. My return flight to New Zealand was delayed. Alone in my hotel room, I slipped in the bath as I reached for my towel. I fell face first towards the tile floor over the rim of the tub. The instant before I landed was as drawn out and full of fear as the moment before Jake's car collided into mine. I managed to break my fall but lay naked and sobbing half in and half out of the tub. I felt my aloneness and vulnerability more acutely than I had before any of my surgeries. The same comforting presence that I met in the car soothed and reassured me. 'It's OK. You're OK.' It was time, finally, to grieve. There was no need to be strong any more. Rather than embrace and comfort this exhausted, vulnerable, frightened part of myself, I towelled off and turned on the television. I couldn't face that much pain after all I'd been through. I thought it would devour me if I let it loose. I could face surgery. But I couldn't face my vulnerability.

Seinfeld cracked jokes as I stared numbly at the television screen. And the angel quietly retreated.

I didn't want to grieve. I didn't want to feel anything but triumphant. I wanted to celebrate. To shout 'I'm back!', as though looking more like my old self would make me that person again. I had already arranged a year of travel to celebrate my 'return'. I was returning to New Zealand only for a few days to see friends before heading to the States to visit family and friends there. Then I was headed to Ecuador with my mother to visit my sister and her husband in the Peace Corps. From there I was going on to Guatemala to visit my other sister Pat and, I hoped, to volunteer my time helping others.

What I should have been doing was resting and letting go

of the tears that I'd held back for so long while I focused on my recovery. I should have been alone or with people who recognised and could be with me in this fragile state with patience and tender compassion. But that wasn't an option. My house was already rented out, my belongings stored, and I was on my way.

I arrived at my friend Loula's house in New Zealand exhausted, bruised, having difficulty walking and even more difficulty getting my bags from the taxi into the house. I opened the door to discover notes pinned to the walls from Loula and her son Yoshka welcoming me back and letting me know that she would be home right after work. I cried, grateful for the welcome and devastated that I was in no shape to celebrate. I wept for an hour as I wandered aimlessly around the empty house, trying to unpack, trying to function, until I finally gave in to my grief and exhaustion and fell into bed with a hot-water bottle for comfort.

I cried for three days. It didn't matter where I was or who I was with. It seemed like there was no stopping it. It was as though I'd reached the finish line of a brutal four-and-a-half-year marathon that took every ounce of strength and focus I had. If I could have, if I was in my own home, I think I would have closed the door and gone to bed for months, maybe forever. I couldn't believe that I had to be ready in five days for an unknown future. In the middle of all this, I was called on to fix the plumbing for my tenants, deal with repairing my car window from a break-in that happened while I was away . . . and I got the first period I'd had in a year! People who'd never seen me cry before were only surprised by the timing, that I'd managed to hold it together for so long.

Before I knew it I was back in the air again for a twelve-hour flight. I landed in California and had an intense visit with some dear friends before climbing into a van with my sister Linda and her kids for an eight-hour drive up the coast to meet my mother for a two-night holiday. The kids played video games the entire way. Then it was my turn to get behind the wheel of my mother's car and drive another eight hours to her home. I was shattered.

I lay awake at night feeling nauseous with exhaustion. So much remained unattended in my inner life — the home of my true self. No one knew I was falling apart. Those I tried to tell didn't believe it. To them, my accident was long over. They had supported me through my recovery and now it was time to move on. Why shouldn't they expect that? I had.

For the first time since she had flown to my bedside following the accident, there was tension in my relationship with my mother. She was eighty-five now and a trip to South America confronted her with her own vulnerability, something that she resented as much as I resented mine. Neither of us could create the atmosphere of excited anticipation that we both wanted to feel. Instead, we bickered with each other until I left for the east coast to visit my brother in New York and friends outside of Boston. The trip was meant to be my opportunity to show family and friends how well I had recovered and to thank them for all their support, a chance to share my victory with them. They were presented instead with a needy creature terrified of driving a car in Boston traffic or of managing with bags I could hardly lift. It wasn't that I didn't want to drive myself back into the city from my friend's beach home. I didn't think I could. I was anything but relaxed, good company, anything but in a victorious mood.

I met my mother in a Florida motel for our flight to Ecuador early the following morning. Up before dawn, we arrived to discover that the flight was delayed six hours. There was no way to let my sister and brother-in-law know. When at last we did arrive, they were there waiting for us with a taxi van. Everyone was tired. My bags were lost by the airline. No one was in a good mood. Mostly it stayed that way. My sister and her husband were finding their Peace Corps experience a great disappointment, as were many of their Peace Corps friends. They weren't happy. They had arranged for my mother and me to stay at a fairly upmarket hotel while they stayed at a cheap backpacker hotel nearby to save money. I wasn't happy about that. So it went . . . The pool in the cruise boat we took to the Galapagos Islands had no water in it. A fire broke out in the cabin Mom and I slept in. My mother's return flight was delayed, no one knew for how long. She was returning alone and nervous about having to make connections in Spanish-speaking countries, or even possibly getting stranded alone in a foreign airport. No one was happy about that. Alternative plans had to be made.

Once we safely saw Mom off, my sister and brother-in-law needed to get back to their village and sent me off to explore Ecuador on my own until we met up for a planned Christmas holiday with a few of their Peace Corps friends. With little more than 'hola' in my Spanish vocabulary, I set off for the Amazon jungle! Looking back now, I can't imagine what I was thinking. Probably that this is what the old Kathy would have done. But I was not that person any more. Crammed into 'chicken buses' as the Ecuadorian countryside flashed by, I couldn't rustle up the enthusiasm I knew should be there. I was numb with exhaustion and, oddly enough, with a vague fear that I wasn't going to be able to cope. Luckily, the part of the Amazon I went to turned out to be nothing like the virgin jungle I had hiked through in Sumatra years before. This was a boat trip and a half-day walk into what amounted to a jungle lodge. It was doable. Just.

I was looking forward to the holiday with my sister and her husband, hoping that the vacation time would ease tensions. It didn't. Just before we were to leave on a twelve-hour bus journey for our Christmas holiday, my brother-in-law blew up at me. That's when I learned that neither he nor my sister were the friends I had always thought them to be.

'How could you possibly believe that we're friends?' he raged at me. 'We see you for a couple of days once a year!'

Was everything I believed to be true, everything I trusted, this fragile? I came to visit them every year. This was my family, people I loved and whom I thought of as friends. I didn't know how much more loss I could take.

Somehow we made it through Christmas. I shut down. Put on a pleasant mask and made conversation. Their friends never guessed that anything was wrong. For the time being my vulnerability was safely hidden from all but me. Locked behind a detached civility, safer but more soul-destroying than open anger ever could be, I was an emotional time bomb.

Next stop, Guatemala.

26

In search of a new life

It feels like a mistake to have tried to come back out into the world to create a new life for myself. It's too hard. People are too hard. And I am too vulnerable.

The day after I arrived in Santa Cruz La Laguna there was a New Year celebration of the foreign community held in the hill top home of my sister Pat. It was the beginning of 1999, almost five years since the accident, five years since this sister that I'd spent my childhood competing with for attention had dropped everything to be by my side. It had taken five years and sixteen surgeries to regain my function and my appearance. Long enough, I thought, to be ready to create a new life for myself. In that time Pat had created a new life for herself in Guatemala on the volcanic crater lake, Lake Atitlan.

The table was covered in food and drink and the 'extranjeros', the foreigners, dressed gaily in flowing post-hippie wide-legged pants and colourful shirts. Music poured from the stereo and the 270-degree view of the lake, volcanoes and canyon spread out before us. I was enchanted! Atitlan is a crater lake 6000 feet above sea level in the highlands of Guatemala. Ringed by pueblos where the indigenous Mayan Indians live much as they have for centuries, Atitlan is dominated by three towering volcanoes on the southern rim. To the north, the nearly vertical landscape is a patchwork of corn fields or milpas and coffee trees. The rugged mountain peaks rise above this patchwork floating in the mist. Hand-carved canoes, or kuyukas, carry fishermen hoping to catch the day's meal as women dressed in traditional costumes of brightly woven cloth make their way along the steep paths carrying bundles on their heads and babies in slings on their backs. I thought I had landed in Paradise!

The foreigners living there were friendly and welcoming to me. All were well travelled, well educated and financially secure. Most were in their forties to sixties. Some had retired or semi-retired early. Others bought and sold Guatemalan crafts for a living. Some ran the few small backpacker hotels in Santa Cruz. Almost everyone practised some art form — writing, screen printing, photography, weaving, painting, and pottery. These were not the young new breed of travellers I met on my journey in 1990, those in search of the next high or the next party regardless of where they happened to be in the world. These were my kind of people! Or so I thought ...

Directly across and slightly higher than my sister's home stood the pueblo of Santa Cruz La Laguna. Mud brick homes and mountains of plastic rubbish that blew in the wind. Emaciated dogs, tails tucked submissively between their hind legs, roamed the dusty streets. Runny-nosed children played in the town square with bottle caps or discarded metal tubes. The boys wore worn-out second-hand clothes from the Salvation Army, though the girls continued the tradition of wearing only the 'tipica', the traditional woven costumes that identified them as Cruzianas, girls from Santa Cruz. Surrounding them was the same breathtaking view as that from my sister's house. Laughter rang out from the children at play as their mothers pounded their washing in the communal washtubs. Self-important, though poorly educated, men filled the municipality building and antique statues of the saints, paint worn away from years in the damp and darkened church, stood guard over the pueblo from the church across the square. The lives of these two very different races of people, Caucasians from Europe and North America and the Mayans indigenous to Guatemala, were both separate and interconnected in ways I couldn't begin to understand.

'Stand on your own two feet' has always been something of a motto in my family. Pat had invited me to visit her in Santa Cruz knowing that I was feeling lost in New Zealand where my friends led busy lives that I couldn't keep up with any more. She was in love with Santa Cruz and had boasted that here the majority of foreign residents were in their forties to sixties, independent, interesting, and living at a slower pace. 'You'd really love it here!' she'd claimed. I needed a new life, one that didn't define me as an accident victim and patient, one that didn't constantly remind me how different I now was. I wanted to be among interesting people who moved at my pace. And I wanted my status back. Soon after I decided to accept her invitation, Pat wrote to say that I should plan to be independent of her. She was not interested in doing 'tourist things'.

She and her partner cooked food bought fresh from the market each night and I did what I'm best at in the kitchen — the dishes — before retiring early to bed in a separate guest house to give them (and myself) some personal space alone. They carried on with their normal activities during the day and I joined in when I could. The rest of the time I did my best to find my way around — to 'stand on my own two feet' and to make friends with the people from the party who had invited me to visit in their homes.

After a week in Santa Cruz as Pat's guest, I gathered the courage to head out to Antigua for two weeks to study Spanish. Antigua is a beautiful Spanish colonial city two and a half hours from the lake. It's famous for its many beautiful colonial ruins, restaurants and tourist shops and for the many Spanish schools located there. I spoke almost no Spanish. Other than tourist phrases — 'Where?', 'How much?', 'Too much!', 'Hello', 'Goodbye' and 'Thank you' — I was incapable of communicating in any meaningful way. So, off I went to begin my new life by learning a new language.

I decided to travel by a local 'chicken bus' — a once yellow school bus from the USA now brightly painted in multi colours — rather than take the shuttle bus that was exclusive to tourists because of its cost. Chicken buses, so-named because live chickens from the market are frequently on board, carry as many as five people in seats designed for two school-age children. The aisles are inevitably filled with people balanced on one buttock on the edge of a seat, with travelling salesmen hawking their wares, and with the unfortunates who are left standing and jostled at every one of the frequent stops as even more passengers get on. All it takes is one trip on a chicken bus, passing traffic on bald tires at breakneck speeds around blind corners, to understand the preponderance of religious decals that adorn them, decals declaring 'Criste es mi amigo' (Christ is my friend) or 'Jesus es amor' (Jesus is love).

I attended Spanish school four hours a day, one-to-one with the teacher, and lived with a family that spoke only Spanish. When planning this trip, I had been confident that total immersion in the Spanish language would have me fluent in no time. How wrong I was! My teacher spoke no English, but he spoke Spanish slowly and carefully using a few nouns and regular verbs in first person, present tense with lots of hand and face movements. I understood immediately! Encouraged, I 'spoke' about politics, economy, and cultural differences in my very limited way. He seemed to understand! But back out on the street and with the family, my attempts to communicate the most simple things were met with furrowed brows and a slight tilt of the head. The family spoke nothing but proper Spanish. At top speed. They used every tense, every colloquialism, and every irregular verb available! Every sentence sounded like one long word. A dictionary in hand, I begged, 'Despacio por favor!' (Slowly please!) But, to no avail. Only my teacher seemed to understand me. That's what he was paid for.

By the end of two weeks of total immersion in the Spanish

language, I needed a break! I returned to Santa Cruz to look after Pat's house and dogs for five days while she and her partner chartered a sailboat on the coast. It was a wonderful opportunity to experience what life in Santa Cruz might be like as a local rather than a visitor. As I sat staring at the beauty that surrounded me everywhere I looked, I began to dream of buying land and of making the new life I so desperately wanted right here in Santa Cruz!

I'd never planned to live in Santa Cruz. I had originally planned to volunteer in an orphanage in a remote village somewhere. But, after two weeks of intensive Spanish classes, I began to remember how little French I knew after four *years* of studying it in high school. How could I venture off alone to a remote region where no one spoke a word of English? Why not live right here and help these people? I dreamed of living in this idyllic place while helping the people in the pueblo. I didn't really understand that, to many of the villagers, my life in New Zealand represented their version of Paradise. A life that was, to them, abundant wealth and freedom — something out of their reach. I was so overwhelmed by the possibility that my version of Paradise might actually be within my reach that I didn't see the potential resentment that our relative wealth, retired lifestyles and even our eagerness to 'help' might create. I didn't recognise that Paradise is more than a beautiful place. It is a state of mind. And this wasn't Paradise for them. We are all equally blinded by our own images of 'Paradise' — a beautiful or wealthy exterior — without any real knowledge of what might lie beneath the surface.

When Pat returned from her sailing trip, I was already

deeply infatuated with Santa Cruz and my budding dream of creating a new life there. It was a dream I couldn't realise without her approval. I knew that. This was a small community and she had already created her own home here. We seemed to have gotten along well and her friends had given me a warm welcome. So I asked her how she would feel if I bought land there. She said yes! Perhaps she felt she had no choice, though I had assured her that I respected her prior claim to Santa Cruz. I ignored the niggling fear that I was probably too fragile to cope with volunteering alone in an isolated part of Guatemala anyway. I was going to create a wonderful new life for myself! Pat stipulated that she didn't want any obligation to 'feel responsible' for me nor to be involved with my purchase of land, which can be quite complicated in Guatemala. For that she referred me to her friend 'Brad', a long-time American resident of Santa Cruz.

Excited, I asked if I could stay at her house a few more days so we could see the land I was interested in together. I offered to go to a hotel if she needed more personal space, but she agreed. So, I was surprised when she returned to the room a few minutes later and announced that yes, she did want me to go to a hotel. But she didn't stop there. She continued on to say that I had 'overstayed my welcome'. I was hurt and confused. I'd stayed with her for only one week in total, although I'd been in the country for a month. I'd paid my way and made sure to give her plenty of personal space. What had I done wrong? I felt like a dog cowering and wagging its tail at the same time. So unsure of — and frightened by — this unanticipated attack. The memory of my brother-in-law's unanticipated outburst in Ecuador was still raw. Why hadn't I seen it coming? I had only 'face value' to gauge what was real and what was not in my relationships. Frightened and hurt by Pat's attack, I hid my own feelings behind a mask — as I had done in Ecuador — and moved into a local hotel.

I suspect now that Pat's outburst had more to do with the prospect of me actually living in Santa Cruz than it had to do with my staying in her house a few days more. But she had agreed and I had accepted that at face value. I was to learn a lot about the risks involved in taking things at face value in the months and years ahead as I struggled to create a new life in a deceptively beautiful paradise.

The local Mayans couldn't imagine why Pat's sister was staying in a hotel. It became a source of embarrassment to her, and to me — a loss of 'face'. From then on it seemed to me that everything I did was a potential source of embarrassment to my sister, who took on 'feeling responsible' for me whether I liked it or not. On some level I knew that it was crazy to believe that I could live in Santa Cruz without living in my sister's shadow, or that, regardless of what she said, she would not resent me for the invasion that my presence seemed to represent in her life. I suppose I didn't want to know.

27

Tortilla tyranny

At the beginning of every American football season, cartoonist Schultz ran the same story line in the Charlie Brown comic strip. Lucy holds the football in place and invites Charlie to kick off the season. 'Come on, Charlie Brown,' she cries. 'Kick the ball!' He holds back, though you can see the eagerness in his eyes. 'You're just going to pull the ball away,' he ventures. 'Charlie! Would I do that?' replies Lucy. 'Come on,' she tempts. 'You know you want to Charlie Brown! Kick the ball!!' Every year Charlie's yearning to believe Lucy wins out and he goes for it. He sprints for the kick-off with everything he has. And every year, at the very last moment, Lucy triumphantly pulls the ball away and Charlie falls flat on his back. Every year he is as amazed as the year before. Poor old Charlie Brown!

I forged ahead towards claiming my own place in Paradise. I was happy to pay Brad US$300, to negotiate the purchase of the property and to make sure that I wasn't cheated. It's not unusual in Guatemala for the same piece of property to be sold more than once — by the same person — to different buyers. A Mayan organisation had plans to build a private 'Basico' or secondary school away from the pueblo, amongst the foreign houses. It was the first time since the foreigners had come to live in Santa Cruz that what would normally occur in the pueblo was to take place where the foreigners lived. It was a contentious issue among the foreigners. Some of those living nearby were fearful of extra noise and rubbish, while those living at a distance were mostly in support of the idea. The school was to be directly behind the property I wanted to buy and had no lake access other than through foreign-owned land. That too was an issue. They were demanding access through people's private property.

The property I wanted to buy was on the lake front. It and the neighbouring property were owned by Guatemalan businessmen, who refused access from the lake to the proposed school. Brad suggested that if I bought the property and gave the school land for a public right of way, I could help them and, at the same time, endear myself to them. They would want to 'bend over backwards' to be good neighbours, according to Brad, and the problem would be solved for all. I was glad to offer land for a public path along the side of my property, but reluctant to sacrifice my privacy. So I offered the school land for a right of way on the condition that they would provide the labour to build a wall for my privacy. I would provide all of the materials. I wanted to establish as equitable and mutual a relationship as possible, as a neighbour rather than white benefactor. The director of the school agreed and I pursued the purchase of the land in earnest with this added goal in mind. What a great beginning it would be for my new life in Paradise! It never occurred to me to get it in writing.

The 'vendador', or seller, was a Latino businessman from the capital city with an overhanging belly and open contempt for the indigenous. He arrived late for our meeting to negotiate the sale accompanied by a woman whom he announced proudly to Brad was twenty-five years younger than himself. I sat through the meeting as mute and invisible as this young mistress as 'los hombres' bantered in Spanish. The landowner held firm to his price and refused to accompany us to the site to physically point out the boundaries. But we did eventually at least get to look at the title and write down the measurements of the land.

Measurements finally in hand, my trusted advisor, Brad, arranged to have the ex-mayor of the pueblo (a powerful Mayan man whom Brad knew well) accompany us to confirm the boundaries of the property. Oddly (I thought), the measurements of the rear boundary wall didn't correspond at all to those on the 'escretura', or title, and stood a good eight metres in front of a large tree the owner had said marked the rear boundary. Brad and the ex-mayor brushed those facts aside and insisted that I accept the wall as the boundary. Then Brad instructed me to give the ex-mayor Q50 — only about NZ$17 at the time, but more than a full day's wage for most men in the pueblo — for a half-hour of his help. I complied, though, in the face of this discrepancy, I wondered just who the ex-mayor and Brad were actually helping.

I went back alone later and measured the land from the tree the seller said marked his rear boundary rather than from the wall. The measurements from there matched the title exactly! Brad was non-committal and seemed slightly impatient when I told him this, although the difference amounted to a good 96 square metres of land. The lawyer assured me that the title, rather than the wall, defined where my boundaries were. So I went ahead and made arrangements for the money to be sent by courier to Guatemala City, where the papers would be signed. Brad, my paid advisor and protector for a problem-free purchase, said he was too busy to attend the signing. So I prepared myself to venture off alone, without understanding of the language, to a city three and a half hours away that was renowned for its dangers, to complete the deal.

The night before I left for the signing, Brad came to see me with an entire committee from the Basico, including his friend the ex-mayor, to inform me that a public path previously existed on the property and that I was required, by law, to give up a one metre wide right of way from the lake front to the school. No wall would be built as had been promised. No concessions made. They made it clear that if I didn't give the land, they would take it. In the two months leading up to this moment no mention had ever been made of a pre-existing path. Mayan acquaintances later told me that no such official path ever existed.

Brad urged me to agree. It was the law, he said. 'Just give it to them!'

The ex-mayor and committee smiled appreciatively at

Brad, who seemed quite pleased with himself.

'Tell them that by all means I will honour their law,' I told Brad. Whose side was he on? When they left I cried. I felt manipulated and bullied. It seemed to me that Brad was using me to win favour with powerful people from the pueblo. It began to seem that I could trust no one, not even the person I was paying to protect and guide me. That very little here was as it seemed on the surface.

It wasn't too late to back out, but I convinced myself that it was. I couldn't let Paradise be snatched from me at the last moment. I wanted to believe in Paradise, in a perfect ending to my journey, no matter how unlikely that was beginning to look.

My lack of Spanish turned out to be the least of my problems in the city. The cheque didn't arrive in Guatemala on Thursday, as arranged by the courier service, nor to me by Friday when the papers were to be signed. Suspicious of me, as well as the Mayans, the seller refused to accept my cashier's cheque unless I accompanied him to the bank. Saturday morning found my lawyer, the seller and me all breathlessly waiting for the courier to bring the cheque before the banks closed. The lawyer typed up a new title — in Spanish — and gave me a photocopy in exchange for US$45,000 (more than NZ$90,000 at the time). A photocopy didn't seem very official, but the lawyer assured me that this was how things were done. We made it to the bank at the last possible moment. Then the lawyer and I began the three-and-a-half-hour trip back to Panajachel. I was feeling none of the joy that I had hoped for. Instead, I kept hearing the words of my older brother who had arranged for the money to be sent to Guatemala. 'Are you sure you know what you're doing? Make sure you get the proper documentation before you hand that much money over.' Could I trust even my lawyer here?

Somehow the lawyer missed the turnoff to Panajachel and we were more than an hour further down the road before he noticed. It was dark and there were almost no other cars on the road. Few, I'd been told, were willing to risk an encounter with 'banditos' on the roads after dark. I held my breath, thinking of the horror stories I'd heard of road-side robberies. People who had cars were, by definition, rich. It was not unusual to hear of bandits blocking roads at night to rob and sometimes kill their victims. Tourist 'shuttle buses', vans known to carry tourists for seven times the cost of travelling by chicken bus, were the most common victims of road-side robbery. A van full of rich tourists was a red flag attracting angry 'bulls' with machetes. Once again, I felt vulnerable and on guard.

But, at last the land was mine! I convinced myself that it was meant to be. The worst was over. Now came the excitement of creating a garden in my piece of Paradise. I bought trees and hired someone to start planting right away.

As I decided where to plant trees on my land and tried to imagine them fully grown, a Mayan man approached me saying that the land between the tree at the rear boundary and the wall was his. A dictionary always at hand, I asked if we might both look at our titles together with a lawyer, which I would pay for. According to my title the land was clearly mine. The Mayan refused to produce any papers, saying only that he 'didn't want problems', an expression I would hear often in Guatemala, which basically translates as 'don't mess with me'. I discovered much later that it was he who had built the wall forward of the true boundary and claimed the excess land as his own while he was 'guardian', or caretaker, of the property for the previous owner. The 'witness' who signed this unofficial subdivision was another man from the pueblo whose own property would also increase in size by moving the boundary. I believe the ex-mayor would have known all of this when he 'helped' to point the boundaries out to me.

To my mind this was evidence of a divide between foreigner and indigenous. Between the 'haves' and 'have-nots'. Was it also evidence of the opportunism of Brad using that divide to his own advantage, to take sides in the unspoken 'them against us' by using me — and my trust — to secure his own tenure in Paradise? I didn't know. What I did know was that the school I had offered 100 square metres of land to in exchange for creating a wall along their path had forcefully claimed that land for a public path, that another local man was claiming 96 square metres more of my land, and that his 'witness' had received yet another piece of my land.

28

Despair

I am firmly attached to fear that nothing is safe.
That the potential for loss is everywhere. That
there are no answers, nothing secure. So I live
in a state of perpetual cringing anticipation of
unseen dangers. Like I am still in the moment of
bracing myself in some stunned, breathless state
of disbelief.

When I was in therapy, I often compared my situation to climbing a steep mountain. I was too exhausted to reach the safety of the hut before nightfall and feared that I would be stranded alone in the dark. My therapists urged me on. How might I make it to the hut? What's stopping me? All I wanted was not to feel so all alone in this dark place. I needed someone willing to be with me exactly where I was. Not to fix me or label my problem. Certainly not to judge or dismiss my experience. Then, as now, I needed someone to sit with me in the dark. Someone who wouldn't run away, insisting that I be stronger than I knew myself to be.

Before I knew it, the rains came and the majority of foreigners left. I rented a very basic little house not far from my property where I designed a small one-room 'casita' or cottage, working by candlelight late into the night. It wasn't long before I discovered that decisions normally left up to an architect, to town planners and the contractor were left up to me . . . Where to put the septic tank, how large I wanted it to be, where to place the water tank and how high, whether I wanted metal reinforcement in the foundation and how much, what angle the roof should be at, etc. An American builder living in Santa Cruz warned that I should have metal reinforcement in the foundation because of frequent earthquakes. I rushed with my dictionary to my contractor.

'¿Hay rebar en el fundación? [Is there rebar in the foundation?]' I asked.

'No es incluido en el precio [It's not included in the price],' he replied.

Meanwhile the rain poured down and the level of the lake rose by almost one metre. All along the shoreline, wherever there were no retaining walls, land was washed away by pounding waves from the prevailing winds. Before my foundation was complete (with rebar!) at least a metre of land along the full length of my waterfront fell into the lake! I had a retaining wall built, guaranteed to last twenty years. The wall didn't last two months! Pounding waves sucked the sandy soil from behind the rocks until there was nothing left holding the wall up! I had it rebuilt — by someone else.

As the rains fell and the wall fell and the construction plodded on 'poco a poco' (little by little) I busied myself with establishing a garden. I took cuttings from friends' gardens of coleus, begonia, ferns, impatiens, poppies, chrysanthemum, geranium, salvia, and whatever else I could find. I spent hours, days, clearing rocks away so that roots could take hold and then I simply stuck the cuttings directly in the ground. The larger rocks from my land formed the foundation of the house and the retaining walls, while huge, flat rocks were put aside for a stone stairway leading from the water to the entrance to my property. This I loved. Designing my house and creating my gardens were a joy.

But earthquakes shook me awake at night. The river flooded, destroying properties. There were landslides. The rain was relentless, as was my diarrhoea. I had to search my bed for scorpions before climbing in. And I worried about making decisions that I was ill-equipped to make.

Feeling isolated as well as overwhelmed by what I had taken on, the earth literally gave way under my feet one day. Early one morning as I made my way to the building site, the sodden, eroded lake-front path collapsed underfoot and fell into the lake, taking me with it. Nothing felt safe or trustworthy any more, not even the ground I stood on. I was in a state of constant alert and near panic. My dream was turning into a nightmare. I was living in a larger house now. One on the isolated far end of Santa Cruz where most of the other houses were closed up for the rainy season. I was far from the village and far from the tourist hotels. There were no phones and only enough solar power for a few lights. Every day I scrambled over rocks and waded across the fast-running river to visit my property or to catch the boat to town for supplies. When the river flooded I stayed put. It became more difficult each day to convince myself to get out of bed. It seemed that every day presented me with more problems to be solved. Problems that, without a grasp on the language or culture, I felt at a loss to resolve. I found that I couldn't concentrate. Couldn't work out the most simple calculations.

I was in trouble emotionally and I knew it. Looking out at the unspeakable beauty of Lake Atitlan, I thought only 'Who cares?' I was more than unhappy. I was seriously depressed. Thoughts of suicide were a strange source of solace to me. Knowing that I didn't have to feel this way forever — that I had the option of ending my life — was the only thing left that I felt in control of. It was the only way I knew how to 'just get over it'. On moonless nights I would imagine swimming as far out into the lake as I could. Without street lights or electricity, there would be no way to make out the shore. The lake was very deep. Those who would suffer as a result of my death could believe that it was an accident. Having that option was somehow comfort enough. I didn't have to act on it.

I tried to share what I was feeling with someone I trusted. She told me that she thought I 'enjoyed' feeling this way, that I got something out of it. She meant well, I knew. She wanted me to get over it. But, from where I stood, that was probably the most stupid thing I'd ever heard. Rationalising someone else's pain away benefits only the person who feels powerless to help. No one ever wants to feel the way I did then. I knew that to get over it I had to go through it.

I stopped trying to talk about my feelings and did the best I could to cover up or hide. I isolated myself more or less until one day my sister and her partner came by for breakfast. Pat seemed to be reaching out, trying to be a good sister, and I was trying to be friends. That morning as I tried to coordinate making eggs, toast and coffee at the same time as I held a conversation, I felt myself begin to panic. It felt like an impossible undertaking! I got them to serve themselves and escaped to the bathroom where, behind the closed door, I clung to the basin and stared in the mirror. What was happening to me? I drew deep breaths into my belly, splashed water on my face and came out with a smile. They asked how the building was going. What was I going to do about this or that. The panic came rushing back and I began to hyperventilate. I was horrified! Pat looked at me strangely.

'What's the matter with you?'

I couldn't speak. I began sobbing. Gulping air. I couldn't stop. Pat jumped up and took me in her arms.

'Oh my God! I know this,' she said. 'You're having a panic attack!' Her partner, a trained emergency medic, got me to breathe into my cupped hands until I was breathing normally again.

'That's it. You're staying with us,' they announced. I wanted their support. I needed help and I knew it. But I was afraid of Pat's anger. Pat started making a list of all that still needed to be done to bring my house to completion. She said she'd handle it. I was afraid of the resentment that I knew I'd face for accepting her help. She'd made it clear that she didn't want to be responsible for me yet I clearly wasn't coping. For months Pat had impatiently insisted that I 'just get over it!' She wanted me to be happy, even grateful for my life. But I wasn't ready for that. The pressure to wear a happy face, to be strong and independent when I was none of those things, only added shame to my growing depression.

I found a doctor in the capital, who told me that my problem was hormonal. He put me on HRT, told me to pray to Jesus, and assured me that I would be feeling like my old self within two weeks. Two weeks later I found myself crying even in public. As soon as I could, I made my escape from Paradise.

My house in New Zealand was still occupied by tenants when I returned. But a friend had gone overseas and offered me his place while he was away. A year had passed since my final surgery in Australia. The emotions that I refused to deal with then hadn't disappeared. They never do. I couldn't hold them at bay any longer. I tried. But when I got back to New Zealand, my tenant moved out unexpectedly and the person who was looking after the house for me quit. I needed to organise maintenance on the house and find new tenants in a short period. Even without the language difficulties, it felt insurmountable. Everything felt insurmountable. My doctor put me on antidepressant medication. Within a few days of taking the medication I was rocking myself and crying on the floor. I thought I was losing my mind! It felt as if someone else was occupying my body. It was a chemically induced 'bad trip'. I literally crawled to the phone and dialled my best friend. I managed only her name before convulsive sobs took over again. Within minutes she was there on the floor with me, holding me while I sobbed over and over, 'I can't.

I can't.' I didn't feel like I could do another thing. I was so tired of being strong!

Another good friend had gone through a similar emotional collapse after the birth of her baby. Formerly a competent television executive, she had found herself sitting on the floor crying in the middle of tidying up her toddler's toys one day. She couldn't cope with anything and she couldn't understand why. Depression is a chemical thing. It is humbling to experience the extent to which we are controlled by chemical reactions in our bodies. Every woman who has experienced PMS knows what I'm talking about. Everyone who ever took illegal drugs, or even got drunk, knows the impact that chemicals can have on our feelings and behaviour. My friend's depression was a result of hormonal changes in her pregnancy. Mine was from having remained in a chemical state of alert from the trauma of the accident and all of the surgeries that followed. After a while my body responded to every challenge as an emergency. I was literally in a constant state of high anxiety for six years. It had finally taken its toll on me.

The doctor changed my medication to one that treats anxiety as well as depression and within weeks the state of high alert I had been living in for so long disappeared. I was so grateful to be free of the protective armour I had worn for so long, feeling that I had to protect myself in a dangerous and untrustworthy world, that I wanted to get down on my knees and thank God. That's exactly what I did. Although I hadn't been to church for thirty years or more, I knocked on the door of a local church and asked to be let in. In the ritual space of the church, with its stained-glass windows, candles, flowers and pews all facing the cross, I knelt and said thank you to a very different God than the one I had known in my church-going years. This one was my friend. It was what connected me to my world, for better or for worse.

Three months later I returned to Santa Cruz! I blamed my inability to cope with the building decisions, the earthquakes, the landslides, the floods, the false claims on parts of my land, my sister's resentment and constant pressure to wear a happy face all on post-traumatic stress and menopause. I wanted to believe that Santa Cruz was the paradise I fell in love with. After five years and sixteen operations, I figured I deserved to have a new life that would make it all seem worthwhile. I deserved Paradise!

29

Paradise found

It feels like this year will be a time of major change.
Perhaps that's just hope talking again. But the more
I give into the dark and scary places, the more I feel
some metamorphosis — something both stronger
and softer emerging.

So, back I went ready to take my place in Paradise. I packed my music, my books, my laptop, a first-aid kit . . . and my antidepressants! I bought sheets and towels, loose-fitting pants, and a new rain poncho. These I carefully packed around my new solar panels, my personal splurge, for my tiny house. No candles for me. I was going to have lights and music and power for my computer. My sister had overseen the final stages of completing the house. Encouraged by her emails about how nice the house turned out, I filled my heart again with hope, bought myself a copy of *501 Spanish*

Verbs and once again said my goodbyes to my New Zealand friends.

There stood my little house just as I had imagined it. Eighteen-and-a-half by twenty-one feet with a six-foot-deep verandah. My caregiver had planted a lawn by cutting single lengths of crab grass and planting each length individually in rows by hand! Where once were piles of rocks was now a rolling lawn and a stone path leading up to the house. The plant cuttings that I had pressed into the wet earth during the rains had been transformed into a lush garden. It was magnificent! All I wanted or needed was in this small living space with its expansive view in every direction. This would be my haven. My retreat. Jubilant, I threw open the door to the house . . . and saw that the building dirt had not been cleaned up, the bed had not been assembled and there was no gas for the stove.

My young Mayan caretaker, Anastacio, bought a full gas tank for me while I swept up and assembled my bed. Then I boiled pasta, heated sauce from a jar and we dined sitting on the tiled floor of my new house. This has always remained a special memory for Anastacio and me. He'd never been invited to a meal inside a foreigner's house before and it mattered not one bit to him that, without furnishings, we dined sitting on the floor. My arrival represented new beginnings for him too. At nineteen he was 'guardian' of a foreigner's property, a much sought-after position and a promotion from the position of 'ayudante' (helper) to my sister's guardian. Nor did it matter to me that it was with this relative stranger that I celebrated my arrival in my new home. He was genuinely excited by my arrival and as eager as I for a happy future together.

That year was the beginning of the new millennium and of a new, post-accident victim, post-surgical patient life for myself. With the house completed, it was a time I devoted to establishing my garden and my relationships in Santa Cruz. The garden was the easy part, even with the 'sanpopos' (cutter ants) marching away with entire plants overnight! To my utter amazement, everyone in Santa Cruz seemed caught up in daily busyness, just as they were at home. Social get-togethers were organised events rather than a simple matter of popping in and hanging out with one another. It's not at all my style to host formal dinners or throw parties. So, like in New Zealand, I slipped into a more or less solitary lifestyle at my own pace. I got into a routine of gardening, reading, writing, taking care of the shopping and correspondence in Panajachel twice a week, and going to bed early. The big difference between a quiet existence in Santa Cruz and in my city home in New Zealand was knowing that when I turned off the lights at 8.30 at night in Santa Cruz and looked out my window, most of my neighbours' lights were out also. I didn't feel conspicuously on the outside as I did in my other world where everyone was racing through life at a pace I neither could keep up with nor wanted any more. Only one person in Santa Cruz knew the person I was before the accident. I had imagined that would ease the pressure I felt in New Zealand to try to be someone who no longer existed. Instead, I found that because I was Pat's sister, I experienced even more pressure to be someone I wasn't.

Because I lived in the southern hemisphere, where the seasons are the opposite of the northern hemisphere, my chosen time for coming to and leaving Guatemala was almost opposite to that of my neighbours, who came in November and left with the rains in May. I arrived in February, feeling as if I was arriving at a party at midnight and stayed until August, long after most of the party guests had left! During the rainy season (which corresponds to the rainy season in New Zealand) I found Santa Cruz a far more intimate place to live, with only a few foreigners remaining and social contact on a more personal scale. With the rain, the parched dry hills turned into a verdant green patchwork of milpas (corn fields) and coffee trees and my garden was a joy. The days begin with sunny skies during the rainy season. If you time it right you can get to Panajachel for the market, bank, and Internet café and back, or you can clear the soft wet earth of weeds, before the rain arrives between 1 p.m. and 3 p.m. Evenings often provide spectacular light shows as electric storms on the coast light up the sky, silhouetting the volcanoes. With the rain come the fish. Men and boys huddled against the rain under plastic sheets grub for insects as bait and, using only an empty tin can wrapped in fishing line with a hook, go in search of dinner. I watch from my porch with a cold bottle of 'Gallo', the local beer.

I loved my new house, my garden, Anastacio, and many of my new friends — Mayans and foreigners alike. The views were so stunningly beautiful that I often would whisper to myself as I sat on the verandah gazing at the volcanoes, 'Look at where you are!' More than anything I loved the pace of my life. For the time being I managed to ignore the claims on my land. One day I would simply build a wall as everyone else did to mark their territory. For now I just wanted to enjoy this beautiful place. To relax, recover, and begin anew.

30

Paradise lost

It is better to be hated for what you are than to be loved for something you are not.
— André Gide

No price is too high for the privilege of owning yourself.
— Friedrich Wilhelm Nietzsche

In Guatemala I was confronted with the kinds of masks that people of different cultures present and the almost impossible task of interpreting those masks accurately. Gringos and Mayans wore different faces as a group — generally one benevolent, and the other deferential — and as individuals within their own group. To create a relationship completely outside one's group identity was extremely difficult, especially where money or power was concerned. Both the benevolence and deference were, for some, simply a means to an end.

By the end of my second year in Santa Cruz, I understood how corrupt the group building the Basico school behind my land was and how unaccountable they were to the Irish charity that had funded the building of the school. The school staff were mostly members of the same family, on whose useless, boulder-filled land, without legal access through neighbouring properties, the Basico was built. They had computers, mobile phones, fax machines, new office furniture, and salaries long before the classrooms, or even the bathrooms, were completed. One even bought himself a boat and a motorcycle — 'for school business' he said. The building supervisor — indeed most of the builders of the school — were from the family or were friends of the family. People from the pueblo as well as foreigners were intimidated by this family. Unlike the vast majority of the people living in the pueblo, they openly hated foreigners. They claimed that even those foreigners who owned land and made their homes in Santa Cruz were outsiders and had no rights. I tried to ignore them. I just wanted to be left alone to enjoy this new life I'd worked so hard to create.

I had given the Basico access to their building site as promised, but they wanted more. By now I knew that I had had no legal obligation to give them any land at all. I let them build a dock and a pump house at the end of the path. They ran their water pipes through my property without asking and stockpiled building supplies there too. I allowed this as well. But when I hired someone from the pueblo to set posts in the ground marking a boundary that gave them a one-and-a-half-metre-wide path, the entire family and Basico committee chased my worker off the land and filled in the holes he had dug. They were there waiting for me when I got back from town with the cement. A few of them were drunk. All were threatening. They already had 150 square metres of my land. They wanted 200 square metres. Mostly, I thought, they wanted to prove that, as a foreigner, I had no rights.

I knew enough Spanish to understand the insults they hurled my way as well as their threats that if I built a boundary wall, they would tear it down. But my Spanish was not good enough to defend my rights with any dignity. The Mayan man working for me was afraid of them and warned me that they were 'mala gente' (bad people). That much I already knew, though it wasn't politically correct to say such a thing about anyone indigenous as far as the foreigners were concerned. He agreed to continue his work after the committee left on the condition that I was present. He warned me that I must not wait to erect a solid cement wall immediately. Other Mayans I knew told me the same. It was their way. But my sister and other foreigners warned me that doing so would only increase the wrath of the Basico. I bought into the fear, had the posts cemented in place to mark my boundary, but didn't erect a wall. I headed back to New Zealand for the summer, thinking that my territory was at least safely established. Big mistake!

While I was in New Zealand, these same people from Bascio openly dug up and moved my boundary posts, helping themselves to more of my land to widen the path I had already given them. When I returned, I was urged by all but one foreigner to ignore the theft and the ultimate insult that it represented. It created a huge uproar from the foreign community, who were afraid of losing their stake in Paradise if I challenged this crime. I didn't understand. Unless they were willing to openly address the threatening posture of this particular group, to insist on mutual respect, their paradise would be no more than a sham. A hotbed of fear and corruption set in a beautiful environment.

A surprising number of foreigners living in Santa Cruz insisted that we were no more than 'guests' there, though I doubt they would have said the same had someone stolen land from them. These same residents were unwittingly helping to support corruption through direct 'donations' given without question or accountability to people that even those in the pueblo feared. Others, well aware of the corruption of those in power, tried to manipulate access to that power for themselves. One American resident told me that she was perfectly willing to 'throw money' at the Basico project if it would secure her place in Santa Cruz. She wasn't interested in the politics of it. She knew that it is exactly this kind of solicitude that helps to create tyrants by refusing to challenge even blatant public abuses of power — especially by those who are masters at manipulating white guilt — but she didn't care. She had the money to keep them on her side. And she was accumulating properties.

It became clear to me that even the pretence of submission to these tyrants would weaken any chance of living together in mutual respect. Many of my neighbours privately said to me, 'You're right. What they're doing is wrong. But I'm not going to risk my neck to support you.' No one wanted to risk their neck. It seemed an odd kind of reverse racism in which the rich foreigners took a submissive posture in order to secure their place in Paradise. Brad even went so far as to say, 'You're going down, girl, and I'm not coming with you.' It was just my bad luck that I was the one whose land this group wanted. I was clearly on my own.

All my life I had shaped myself around what I believed would win me the approval of others. I wanted to be liked. To be accepted. To belong. Who doesn't? I knew the pain of rejection and had taught myself how to more or less avoid it . . . or else be the first one to do the rejecting. But for the years since the accident I had been ruthlessly rejecting myself — because I didn't look like me, didn't feel like me, couldn't do all the things I once thought made me who I was. Now I was facing the possible rejection of almost the entire small community that I lived in and wanted to make my part-time home.

At first I succumbed to the pressure. The mayor of the pueblo threatened that he couldn't 'protect' me if I didn't sign a document saying that I gave the stolen land freely. I decided to just let them have the land and even agreed to have him draw up a document to that effect, which I would sign. Everyone was relieved . . . except me. I despised myself. I cried myself to sleep . . . Then something both terrifying and liberating happened. I realised that being true to myself was more important than being liked! That trading some of my deepest values — including my self-respect — for the approval of others, was something I couldn't live with. I knew that taking legal action against those who stole my property would likely cost me more than the land for the path was worth and that, in the Guatemalan system, I would probably lose. If others were right, I might even be physically harmed or killed for standing up to them (though I didn't think so). I certainly would not be popular with the other foreigners who were adamant that I would ruin it for everyone if I stood up to the people who had so defiantly and publicly stolen my land. That if I laid charges against them, I would be responsible for creating a racial war in this peaceful paradise. Everyone was waiting to see what I would do.

I went to the judge in the pueblo, who was a Mayan woman from another pueblo. She told me that she admired me for standing up for my rights, but that she couldn't help me. I understood that she was there to settle issues between members of the pueblo, not between Mayans and Gringos. Certainly not land issues. I travelled to a small pueblo on the other side of the lake where an American priest had lived and worked for over forty years. The Mayan people loved and respected him, I knew, and he had no agenda of personal gain in his relationship with them. I told him my story and asked for his guidance. He knew the Mayan people better than any of us.

'Everyone is telling me to be afraid, but I can't establish my life here that way. How can I respond to this out of love — for myself and for them — rather than out of fear? What's the right thing to do?'

Father Gregory asked me to be patient while he found out more from his colleagues in the church who were more familiar with Santa Cruz. When, at last, we spoke again, Father Gregory informed me that what I suspected was true — that this family was dangerous. I was unlikely to win and could possibly be at risk. 'Sometimes there is nothing we can do, Kathy.'

I went to the district 'Municipalidad' to explain my situation. No one in Santa Cruz was willing to translate for me, so I hired a tourist to translate. 'What are my rights and responsibilities under the law?' I asked. The law had been broken, I was advised, and I had the right to lay charges. As in New Zealand, there seemed to be some disparity between the traditional indigenous custom and modern-day law, between traditional 'rights' and 'ownership'. As I understood it, traditionally land was owned communally by the pueblo and the sole right to possession and use of land was allocated by the mayor according to need. If the community needed some of the land back for the communal good it could be taken or redistributed. Then money came into the picture. The indigenous now sold the right of possession to land for money, sometimes big money. Modern-day Guatemalan law stipulates that the owner of the 'derecho de posesión', the right of possession, has sole authority over the land. No one can simply take it back.

I knew I couldn't live under the shadow of fear of what my neighbours might do next. People I had only wanted to help and who stole from me in return. I decided to stand up for what I believed in, even if I stood alone and even if it cost me my place in Paradise. As soon as I committed myself to that decision, I rediscovered my self, the 'me' that had been there all along — behind the different faces I had worn, the different lifestyles I had experienced, the different jobs I'd had, and the different roles I'd played in the lives of others. I rediscovered the core person that I valued even more than being liked! The very thing I'd been searching for all along in the mirror, in relationships, in job status, family role, lifestyle . . . The pot of gold at the end of the journey. All that I had lost — physical, emotional, social — the things that I had based my identity on — were the very things that had kept me from knowing who I was at the deepest level. Having lost so much else, I wasn't willing to squander my authenticity ever again for the approval of others. In the end, my dream of Paradise was a small price to pay. Against everyone's advice, I laid charges against the people who had stolen my land. I am only sorry that I failed to notify the mayor that I had changed my mind about signing the land away before I laid charges. For this error, I imagine that he 'lost face' in his own community and I made a new enemy.

I was the topic of gossip in Santa Cruz! Everyone got into the act. The foreigners wanted to call a community meeting and asked me to attend after having made it clear that they didn't support me. I declined. People who had never been on my land showed up to tell me what they thought. Pat begged me not to go through with the 'denuncio', the charges. 'They'll kill you, Kathy!' she wailed. I knew it was hard on her being my sister in that environment. She had started a charitable organisation, 'Amigos de la Escuela', to help the children of Santa Cruz a few years earlier. It was run with donations from foreigners, their friends and families and had been working closely with the primary school in the village to ensure that more children got a decent free education. Decisions on how to spend the money were made together with the teachers and principal and every quetzal (the Guatemalan currency) was accounted for. She was well respected in the community and she deserved it.

There were several 'proyectos' or charitable projects

run by foreigners living in Santa Cruz. One of these projects paid all of the students' fees to Basico without any direct accountability for how that money was spent, even though most of the Basico students were from other pueblos. Santa Cruz students preferred to go elsewhere. I appealed to my sister and to my neighbours who were involved in the projects to make it a condition of support that Basico be accountable for the money they received and that they behave within the law. 'Don't support their corruption. The entire pueblo is watching.' They refused to 'get involved', though they made it clear that they didn't support me.

I stood up to the Basico that year and the next. I paid a lawyer in Guatemala to carry on for me while I was in New Zealand. Nothing got resolved. By the end of my fourth year in Guatemala, I knew that nothing would get resolved either legally or in terms of ever feeling as I once had about Santa Cruz. That love affair was over! I had a few friends left there. Not many, but enough. Pat and I fought and made up more times than I can count. We tried to be friends but there was just too much hurt and resentment.

There were moments after I knew that I would have to sell up and leave, that I sat on my verandah at the end of the day and contemplated the view before me. Moments when the volcanoes were shrouded in a soft mist and the air had an ionic, fresh smell of electricity following a thunderous release of rain. The scent of belladonna flowers, the sound of the crickets and an occasional boat in the distance making its way home all filled me with sadness at the thought of leaving. I sat there and saw before me the paradise I had fallen in love with. Like watching one's lover as he or she sleeps, so perfect in repose that one can easily fall in love all over again, I knew both love and grief. For this perfection, this miracle of beauty and tranquillity — Paradise — was not as it seemed.

Like the 'faces' we wear in the world, 'Paradise' is just another image, behind which lies something far more complex, something whose shadows give it depth while revealing its imperfection. As I have done many times in my life, I saw in Santa Cruz a beautiful image and filled in the details of character with my imagination. This is not the first time that I have been disappointed by the less than perfect nature of reality. Not the first time that I have fallen in love with a dream. A boyfriend once told me that he thought I was more in love with who I thought he could be than with who he was. It took me years to admit, even to myself, that he was right. Except for the brief falling-in-love phase, I was always more in love with how I thought people, places or things could be — myself included — than I ever was with how things actually are. I suppose that I was trying to avoid the kind of suffering that is just part of life by always looking for something more or better. I missed out on a lot that way.

The children who play barefoot in the dusty centre of Santa Cruz had no dreams of life other than as it was and always had been in this isolated village. But the arrival of the foreigners, with their relative wealth and material security, has created a dream born of envy among the indigenous, of a different kind of paradise, a material paradise, that they might one day possess. Their image of a perfect life — Paradise — is as unrealistic, as naively idealistic as my own. It is as obvious to me that material wealth can't protect us from suffering as it is to them that living in a beautiful place isn't what Paradise is all about. Clinging to such dreams can result in an anger and frustration so fierce that we each, in our own ways, become more, rather than less, impoverished.

It was not because Santa Cruz is not the paradise that I had imagined it to be that I decided to leave. I had to go because I didn't know how to live with the reality of corruption and fear that had claimed its place in Paradise long before I arrived, without becoming part of it myself. I found a real estate agent, put up a 'For Sale' sign and said my goodbyes, not only to Santa Cruz la Laguna, but to my attachment to something called 'Paradise'. To the search for perfection — in myself and in others.

Pat and I have discovered that we aren't really friends and aren't likely to be. But we are sisters and always will be. She dropped everything and came to New Zealand when I had my accident and I know I'd do the same. Families bring out all kinds of emotions. Particularly when they are the only family you have. She helped me to realise that I can't rely on my place in the family for security or definition any more than I can rely on anyone or anything outside of myself to tell me who I am and make that feel OK. There is probably no place in the world where we seek acceptance as much as we do within the family. Sometimes we have to let that go in order to know and accept ourselves.

31

Return

I find that I am almost frighteningly content lately with my own company and the pace of my life these days. I had this realisation recently that this 'being in limbo' that I found such a struggle (and such a sense of failure) is just a negative way of looking at being in the moment (which feels more like an accomplishment!). It's not just a matter of changing my mind or convincing myself to look at things differently. That hardly ever works for me. It was more like I had this realisation that sort of snuck up on me when I wasn't looking so that I couldn't quickly reason my way out of it. It fits. Gone is the wall I keep banging my head against.

When I returned to New Zealand I knew for the first time since my arrival in 1974 that I was home, that I was through looking for something more or better while missing out on where I was. New Zealand is not the unspoiled place that I once thought it was, but I wanted to kiss the ground when I arrived back. Most of my New Zealand friends grew up at a time when almost everyone was expected to do their OE, their overseas experience, before finally coming home to settle. Many travelled the world. Some went to other Commonwealth countries to live and work. Almost all recall wanting to kiss the ground when they finally came home. New Zealand was, and still is, an exceptional place to live. It too was a paradise to me when I arrived almost thirty years ago.

Since then I have watched it change from a materially egalitarian social democracy to a free-market economy that has brought more wealth to some and more poverty to others than New Zealand had ever before experienced. For years I had felt cheated out of Paradise. I resented the steady erosion of the quality of life in New Zealand as it became more complex, more competitive and more acquisitive. I decried the worldwide lack of any place left that was 'unspoiled'. Until I found — and once again lost — the very notion of Paradise in a small Guatemalan village.

I had spent most of my life, I realised, eagerly pursuing the future or clinging to the past. Rarely appreciating what I had in my pursuit of something better. I have no doubt that has had a great deal to do with why I have always remained uncommitted and single. And, why I yearned sometimes to return to my roots in the United States. Those 'roots', my formative years, were the prevalent culture and values of the sixties and early seventies in the United States. That culture changed long ago, as has the New Zealand culture in more recent years. An entire new generation of New Zealanders has never known the qualities or lifestyle that I fell in love with when I first came to New Zealand — the easygoing, relaxed, neighbourly, safe, trusting, socially conscious, helpful, family-oriented country where there was enough for everyone — including enough time for themselves and for one another. New Zealand isn't perfect. But as soon as I returned I knew just how much I love it, warts and all. Not surprisingly, the values I share with my New Zealand friends are more a reflection of my own than many of those I encountered in Guatemala. I have lived in New Zealand now for more years than I lived in the States.

When I returned, I wasn't surprised to find my friends still living at a faster pace than I. What did surprise me was that I no longer felt the same self-imposed shame that I couldn't keep up with them. A shame I had felt even though I knew that I didn't want to be in the race. I had convinced myself that I was 'boring' because I wasn't as busy as everyone around me. I could see now that when I did have a full-time career and more active social life, my life was no less 'boring' than it is today. It was just more busy. Busy doesn't necessarily mean happy or fulfilled. Sometimes it's just a hiding place from emptiness. The same kind of emptiness you sometimes try to fill up with junk food or shopping for things you don't really need.

I stopped trying to prove my worth — to myself as well as everyone else — by my achievements. I began to appreciate the fact that I could shape my days as I wished, that I could stay up as late as I wanted reading a good book or writing or just watching a good movie on television, that I could garden or dream, and that I could enjoy my own company. That's not to say that I don't sometimes get bored like everyone else. It's more like I've become aware of how interesting even the most simple thing can be — the chorus of birds that wake me in the morning, the kinds of food others in the checkout line are buying, the way I feel in different circumstances. My mother recently told me that she was glad to know that someone else's life was as boring as her own. In many ways her life and my own aren't all that different. We both have creative interests. Mine is writing and hers is photography. Neither of us have much access to friends. Mine are working and raising families and hers are mostly dead. The difference is that her life is 'boring' in part because, at ninety, she has less choice than I do, and mine is 'simple'. It's just a matter of judgement. I figure I've been a harsh judge of myself — and the world around me — long enough.

I still do what I can to change things that I wish were different. Since my return I have been involved in groups and activities trying to address some poorly planned growth that is having a permanent impact on the character of our city. I do what I can. I present submissions to the council on issues I feel most passionate about. I have written and had articles published about issues of current public concern. I march and hand out leaflets and sign petitions. I belong to a local community group. But I don't seem to need to be driven by anger to do those things any more. It's new to me, this fighting without anger. The anger never helped anyway. Sometimes it did more harm than good.

Instead of remaining frustrated with the health system's

apparent disinterest in what I might have to offer (as a psychologist experienced in health care from both sides of the bed) about the potential health and financial impacts of the patient/provider relationship, I decided to learn more about it. One of the first things I did when I returned from Guatemala was to attend classes at the university in health psychology and psychoneuroimmunology. It's been years since I attended university classes. I knew absolutely that the doctor/patient relationship can have an important impact on the wellbeing of both the doctor and the patient, but I wanted to learn how things like stress and fear affect the immune system. I hope to continue to study in this area.

While I was in Guatemala, my next-door neighbour in New Zealand had built an extension to her house right along our common boundary — three feet from my house — on the sunny side. While it was all perfectly legal, where once the sun poured through my lounge and kitchen windows, and bougainvillea tumbled over the fence, the wall of her extension blocked out even a view of the sky. I was devastated. This was my first home and I had spent years of hard work transforming it from a run-down old house into the welcoming cottage it now was. Now that I could no longer retreat from the New Zealand winter, it became a real thorn in my side.

I knew that my home would never see the sun again and that there was nothing I could do to change that. My stomach tightened with anger every morning as I walked into the dark, cold living area. The house was all I had left of the old me. I couldn't give it up. And I couldn't get it back. But since I had left the head-banging behind in Guatemala, I decided to do the same in New Zealand. Within a year of my return I sold the house that had been my home for eighteen years. I have no regrets. I now own an expansive, sunny, open, comfortable home surrounded by mature trees on a private section. It is both a metaphor of the many changes I've undergone and a marker of new beginnings. I feel 'at home' again.

32

Grief — the road to recovery

Not everyone is transformed by grief. But those who dare — or are forced — to be changed in some significant way by their loss, have the opportunity to reap valuable rewards at the end of their journey. In my case, I lost everything that previously defined me. I lost my innocence and the defences that I developed over a lifetime. But in the long personal journey that followed, I recovered much more of myself than I lost. For that I am grateful.

Ten years, sixteen surgeries, and an attempt to create a new life in Guatemala have passed since the accident and the overwhelming loss that began my journey into the underworld of grief. The physical losses — my face and much of my physical functioning — were the most immediate and obvious. Less visible were my loss of innocence, confidence, independence, and the sense of who I was in the world. As time passed, social losses made themselves known. I lost friends (though I made new friends in the process), my professional status and my active lifestyle. Confronting the void that seemed to be all that was left of my life, I fiercely denied the probability that these losses were permanent.

Regardless of what losses take us into our personal underworld, we all share a similar grief process — denial, bargaining, anger, despair . . . and acceptance.

For years I was stuck in denial of the permanent nature of many of my losses. I tried to make myself the same strong, vibrant person I had been physically through physiotherapy, osteopathy, exercise, doctors' visits, and a series of orthopaedic operations. I carried on long after those close to me felt that I should stop and accept my losses. I fought my emotional losses with the same vigour through therapy, medication, journal-writing, meditation and my insistence on remaining authentic even when that was unwelcome and difficult to those around me.

Some forms of denial are both healthy and constructive. It is said that God will never confront you with more than you can handle. I've come to believe that denial, which is part of every grief experience, plays an important role in helping us to grieve loss in doses that we can survive and move through. It was denial that got me through the initial realisation of the full extent of my losses. 'Lost my face, not my spirit,' written in critical care to reassure others that I was OK, was as much a denial of what lay ahead of me as it was an affirmation of my determination to survive.

For each loss I experienced, there came a point where

I could reclaim no more. Before I could accept that I had reached the limit of what I was able to recover, of my life and sense of my self, anger drove me and shielded me from helpless despair — anger at those I was forced to depend on, at my situation and at my self.

When even my anger was not enough to unlock doors to my recovery, I was brought to my knees. I bargained with God. I prayed. I begged. I made promises. It wasn't until I got angry at God for not giving me what I so desperately wanted, that I finally fell into despair. I became alienated from a world that now seemed too fast, too false, too shallow and uncaring. I was exhausted by my efforts to remain strong, independent, successful and in control when none of those things seemed possible any more. I felt isolated even from my own image in the mirror and disempowered by the endless hours I spent waiting as the world outside raced by. Without my former belief that success is a matter of getting things 'right', I didn't know what to be guided by. I was lost. And I railed at God for leaving me 'hanging on a hook', my sense of self decomposing like the piece of rotting meat in the story of Inanna.

I had no preparation before entering this dark place. I had until then outrun any real acceptance of my vulnerability or, indeed, of any other characteristic that didn't fit my image of myself. I needed to allow the death of who I had been in order to free who I might become. But, in order to do that, I had to go into the depths of my being and face the hidden parts of my ego — what Carl Jung would call my 'shadow self' — before I could let it go. It was agonising . . .

While I fought my losses and faced my demons, subtle

changes were going on behind the scenes, hidden even from me. By the time I came to accept that I can't always be strong, attractive, independent, entertaining or even nice, I realised (with delight!) that I didn't want to be! It was only then that I realised that the image I formerly held of myself and so desperately wanted back was a prison of my own creation made up of all the 'shoulds' I had come to believe in. Many of those shoulds, of course, were of value. But, without being confined to a narrow image of what I should be, should do, should think or feel, I was free to choose — to decide for myself moment by moment — all that I could be, could do, could think or feel. I came to realise that looking for my identity in a career, in a relationship, in a family role, in achievements, in my appearance or lifestyle . . . were simply ways of trying to find a new, though still limited, image of myself. A new role to play on the stage of life. Just as trying to replicate the old adventurous me in a new environment was simply a new take on an old image. Everyone of us is more — much more — than whatever it is that we rely on for our identity.

What I needed all along was not to create a new image — a new 'face' — to replace the one I had lost, but to shed any self-limiting image created for the approval of others.

In many ways I succeeded in my determination to reclaim my physical losses, more than anyone expected. In other ways I did not. Physically I am neither particularly strong nor vibrant these days. I can't run or jump, negotiate steep declines without aid, or carry a backpack. But I practise yoga and t'ai chi regularly. It is different kind of physicality. More gentle, more inward. And it suits me.

My attempts to undo my emotional losses helped me to find core parts of myself previously hidden even from me because they were not shaped by the reflections of others. I had been looking in the wrong place for my identity — in the eyes of others. Looking inward, I discovered how much more emotionally complex I was than I had ever known myself to be! And how much more connected I was to others that I might have once thought I had nothing in common with. The old 'me' that I was trying to find was only a tiny part of what I discovered.

Socially, I have fewer friends now and a less active social life. But my need to be popular is gone and my ability to love has grown correspondingly. With the simple recognition that we are all more alike in our common humanity than we may appear to be on the face of things, I'm not lonely any more. I'm neither as passionate nor as emotionally fearful as I once was either. A funny thing about having your worst fear come true (in my case, total dependence) is that whatever we fear loses its power once it becomes a reality.

My professional 'self' seems to be gone. Though I tried hard to get back into the professional arena in my early fifties after several years of recovery, I didn't succeed. I don't have the high profile or salary that I might once have thought I needed to give me credibility in the eyes of others (and myself). What I do have is time, which I have always valued over material possessions. That time isn't spent waiting for anything any more. It was the waiting that was so painful, not the time itself.

After a long, difficult journey through the personal hell of grief, I eventually resurfaced with greater compassion for myself and for others. I discovered that recovering didn't require that I re-cover the fullness of who I am with a limiting new 'face' to present to the world. If ever there was a Garden of Eden, banishment came not only with the shame of realising our nakedness, but with the fear of being judged should we expose the fullness of who and what we really are. Judged not only by God, but by each other. Some socially and self-imposed limits of expression are necessary, of course. We are all capable of the best and worst that we see, and judge, in others. Neither success nor failure can adequately define me. Nor can any loss, however great, diminish who I am. Beyond the masks that others wear, hoping as we all do for approval, I know that the same is true. It takes time, trust and compassion to see beyond the images we each present to the world . . . sometimes even for the one whose image it is.

There is a brokenness
out of which comes the unbroken
A shatteredness
out of which blooms the unshatterable
There is a sorrow
beyond all grief which leads to joy
and a fragility
out of whose depths emerges strength.
There is a hollow space
too vast for words
through which we pass with each loss,
out of whose darkness
we are sanctioned into being.
There is a cry deeper than all sound
whose serrated edges cut the heart
as we break open
to the place inside which is unbreakable
and whole
while learning to sing.

— Rashani